D1825117

Prisoner 4374

Prisoner 4374

A.J. Griffiths-Jones

Only Death Will Find You...

Within the slender boundaries between heaven and hell
Sit all the black angels
This is where we will find you.
Against the shadows on a cold moonlit night
Lie all the forgotten heroes
This is where we will find you.
Behind the gravestones,
Where evil breathes upon the tombs of the innocent
Gloom rears its ugly head.
This is where we will find you.
Where the stench of death prefers to lurk,
Where the good will fear to tread,
Where the Devil eats the souls of men,
Only death will find you.

A.J. GRIFFITHS-JONES

Note from the Author

The events, people and places recounted in these pages are based upon fact. I have chosen the rather unconventional method of writing in an autobiographical style in the hope that the reader can envisage the crimes and consequences that led to the trial of a notorious felon.

Until now, the finer details of Dr. Thomas Neill Cream's life have been, relatively, undocumented. Cream has been branded as a 'Jack the Ripper' suspect since the beginning of the 20th Century, and only now can it be revealed as to whether he earns a rightful place on that suspect list, or not. Over a decade of research in to Cream's life has allowed me to recreate the circumstances of his crimes in considerable detail. In writing his biography I have been fortunate in accessing a number of resources, for which I will be eternally grateful to those who have supported me in pursuit of the truth.

My work includes exclusive, previously unpublished, photograph's of Dr. Cream for which I have personally obtained copyright. I also have permission to use the complete records from his incarceration, totaling 181 pages of authentic reports from which I have been able to piece together his motives and movements both before and during his imprisonment. These documents alone prove, beyond doubt, where Cream was in 1888, the year of the London 'Jack the Ripper' murders.

Firstly, in recognition of my support network, I mention my darling husband Dave, without whom this book would never have seen the light of day. His belief in me has never faltered and for that he has my unconditional love and respect. I also owe my sincere thanks to

Sylvia Caswell, who has relentlessly read and reread my work, giving constructive criticism and support throughout this long and arduous journey, I am proud to have you as my advocate. Appreciation also, to Barry and Karen Williams, and my good friend Bev Williams for their feedback and honest appraisals. John Reinhardt and his team at the Illinois State Archive have been first-rate in helping me to procure and make use of the records at their disposal, I appreciate it. I owe my gratitude to Heather McNabb and colleagues at the Musee McCord Museum in Canada, for aiding my quest to find original photographs of Cream, and then assisting with the legalities of copyright issues. Faye Robinson and Paul Bickley at Scotland Yard have been both professional and encouraging in providing images from the Crime Museum, thank you. Appreciation also to Sophia Brothers, and her department at the Science Museum Group, who have provided me with further images and support. Lastly, but by no means least, I am beholden to Antony Caswell for his brilliant interpretation and graphic design of the cover for 'Prisoner 4374', you did a wonderful job.

I do hope that you enjoy reading the journey of Thomas Cream's life and that I have succeeded in portraying him in his true colors.

A. J. Griffiths-Jones

Contents

1

In the beginning...

If you asked me to pinpoint the moment when it all started, well, that would be a darn hard task.

I guess you could say that my mother's passing was a pivotal time, how that poor woman suffered, but hey, I didn't set out to carve myself a life of debauchery. I used to teach Sunday school for goodness sake, pillar of the community in my younger days. Let's say it kind of just happened. We're talking about nineteenth century America my friend, a fellow had to make ends meet & sometimes it just meant stepping over the line. Don't get me wrong, I'm no criminal, but to finance yourself in a comfortable manner sometimes you had to put your morals to one side, get your hands a little dirty, ruffle a few feathers. I guess you could blame it on the women too, yep, there you go, it was the women who got me into this mess.

I've always had a natural charm with the ladies, must have been a combination of my inherent good looks and smooth Scottish-American tongue, they just dropped at my feet - ha,ha, literally in some cases! Let's see, there was that disastrous relationship with Flora, even ended up marrying that one. Julia came next, the bitch nearly cost me my life, what with her scheming and lies, but we'll talk about that later. Jeez, it still makes me curse at the very mention of her name. The only woman I really ever loved was Laura, how it pains me to think of her sweet young face, but I never really was the settling kind.

I always regarded marriage as a means to an end, wealth being the optimum prize. Anyhow, I'm guessing that you want to know all about those London street-walkers mostly, but you'll have to be patient dear friend, all in good time. I have so much to tell you.

Let's talk about that 'Jack the Ripper' rumor...oh yes, I've read the books. I'm flattered that so many pages have been devoted to my name, there must be ten score and more who think I did it. Have you joined the ranks dear reader?

Well, I certainly had the surgical talent in those days, used to pride myself that I could gut a hog in darn near three minutes. There is also the little matter that the bitches didn't scream isn't there? And I did just happen to graduate with an excellent thesis on chloroform, that sure would knock the whores out cold.

And then there was that guy from the Whitechapel neighborhood, what was his name, George Hutchinson? Says he saw a 'gentleman' with a horseshoe tiepin near the murder scene. Well, you got me there too, worn one of those since my university days. He nearly got my height, even got a good look at the well-groomed moustache. Guess I fit his description pretty neatly didn't I?

Now those English cops were smart, but even they couldn't figure it out. I mean, one 'Ripper' and a whole force of 'Bobbies', maybe they were just looking in the wrong place all along. Or maybe they were searching but not really seeing...Well friend, I could go on, there are things that even the best of them over-looked. I mean, have you ever asked yourself why a fifty-cent a night bitch would be wearing a silk scarf? And they all were you know. Bit of a coincidence don't you think? You could understand a cotton neckerchief tied around their filthy necks, but silk? Some parting gift that was!

Now then, before you get all excited and go telling folk you know who Jack was, you have to solve a riddle. That being the fact that I was holed up in Joliet State Penitentiary during the entire Ripper episode, with not one iota of an impending parole date.

Sure, there were petitions, but the fact remains I was serving a life sentence in 1888. So, how did I get out of that one? Do you reckon

I paid some doppel-ganger to sit in my cell while I dug myself out & high-tailed it to London? Maybe I bribed Governor Fifer to let me out early, ha, ha, sure he would sleep easy at night with that on his conscience! I mean, I did have money despite my delicate predicament, what with my father's death and all, but do you reckon I would line the pockets of some paper-shuffling bigwig in order to stalk hookers in the London fog? Well maybe that's exactly what I did! Or maybe not...

Regrettably my demise was to be with a noose around my neck at Newgate. They dubbed me 'The Lambeth Poisoner', a rather harsh moniker I thought, considering I was doing no more than cleanse your city streets of disease-ridden sluts. Where was the appreciation from your London Borough Council? Nowhere! Instead they locked me in a cold, damp cell & pronounced me guilty of murder. 'Murder'! Darn cheek, didn't even get compensated for the vast amounts of strychnine I had to purchase from the drugstore. That hangman, Billington they called him, went on to tell the tale that I shouted 'I am Jack...' as the trap was drawn. How can he be sure I didn't say 'Bye Jack...' ? I mean, 'Jack' was still walking the streets when they arrested me for those 'other' unfortunate incidents, would have been polite for a gent to say farewell.

Always tickled me that they never asked if I knew him, Jack that is. I mean, come on, there were some mighty fine medical men lodging in the East End in my day, only seems natural that our paths would cross at some point.

Hell, did I hint he was a doctor? Slip of the tongue friend, don't want to give the game away do I? Jeez, you'll all be queueing up at the pearly gates to ask me his name! Well, if you're good & don't judge me too harshly on my actions, I might tell you about my notorious pal. Let's wait and see...

For now let ME hold the limelight, let me tell you what it's like to be driven by a desire so strong that you breathe, eat and sleep revenge. Your dreams of slaughter become intertwined with your waking actions until you neither know if you thought it or did it, wanted it or despised it, regretted it or revelled in it. I am an addict, I am addicted to my own glorious infamy! Let me share it with you...

Sorry, what was I thinking friend, I should introduce myself: Thomas Neill Cream M.D. at your service.

106 Mansfield Street, Montreal

These were my humble lodgings in a brownstone tenement building in 1874.

At 24 years old, I was a handsome young guy, two years into my medical degree at McGill University, when I found myself in dire need of additional funds, so it came to pass that my very first scam was born. Now don't get me wrong, my father sent me a healthy allowance & truth be told, it pretty much covered my daily requirements. What it didn't allow for were the finer things in life that a man of my reputation was drawn to. You know how it is, mixing with gents from privileged families, I had a certain appearance to maintain. Anyhow, let's just say that what my father didn't take into consideration were days out at the racetrack, top quality leather boots and drunken weekends entertaining ladies of the night.

Now before you get thinking I was some kind of gigolo or compulsive gambler, let me tell you that it wasn't only me. Hell, we were all at it, having a good old time in our student days that is. You would only have needed to take a glance at my Graduation photo to see what a bunch of players we were!

Anyhow, as I said, I needed money fast. Debts were gathering & I had a little overseas trip planned. So in September of the aforementioned year, I paid a visit to The Commercial Union of Montreal for the purpose of taking out an insurance policy on my belongings. They gladly obliged & for just a few dollars a month, covered my worldly possessions for the princely sum of $1,000. Maybe I was a little hasty, but I figured I'd let a few weeks pass & then arrange a little 'fire damage' in my apartment. Needless to say the insurance guys were more than a little suspicious & it took me another two months before they finally settled on paying me the paltry sum of $350. Can't say I was overjoyed as my initial claim was for $978.40 but at the end of the day, a few hundred dollars in my pocket for a pile of burned books was a bonus.

Now that should have been my one time crime, but I guess I found it so easy that the lies just kept on coming. I still to this day have no idea where my devilish streak comes from. Born of a god-fearing Scottish family, I was a good son until the bright city lights changed my ways. I wasn't even going to become a doctor until my father convinced me that I had a natural aptitude for treating the sick. Seems quite ironic now though huh?

I'm guessing that you want an explanation for my sudden change in temperament, and I'm not going to fob you off with excuses. However, there was one significant incident that led me along the path of destruction. Again, it can be blamed on the women. Now I say women, but it must have been just one woman who passed on her disease to me, but I'm damned if I can pinpoint who or where. So friend, as bad luck would have it, somewhere in that great Canadian city, in a moment of pleasurable weakness, I contracted syphilis. Yep, as a man of medical means, I really should have known better and protected myself at all costs. But I didn't and I got it.

At first I thought my headaches were caused by late nights and hard study, but then I talked to Charlie Stroud, a fine gentleman & fellow scholar at McGill, who just happened to be putting his brain matter to good use studying venereal diseases. Now Charlie reckoned that eventually I would go crazy, but I never really paid much attention to that part of his diagnosis. Between us we concluded that a mediocre prescription of morphine would keep the headaches at bay & whatever else followed I would deal with in due course.

I can't say that my predicament hindered my progress as eighteen months later, on March 31st 1876, I graduated with the degree of Doctor of Medicine and Master of Surgery. A momentous occasion, for the son of a migrant lumber merchant, wouldn't you say? Now THAT was a day for celebration! After Professor Roddick gave his valedictory address, something about prudence, sobriety & honor I think, we hit the town at full pelt & carried on drinking till dawn.

Having now become a fully-fledged doctor, I then persuaded my father to cover my costs in putting my feet back on British soil, as I planned to enroll on a post-graduate course at St. Thomas's Hospital in South London the following September. This he did & all was going according to plan, until Flora.

Miss Flora Eliza Brooks, was just about the prettiest young lady I'd ever set my eyes upon. We became close very quickly, her being on a visit to Montreal & not knowing many folks down there, I took it as my duty to escort her to dinner & show her the many wonderful sights. It also didn't hurt that her father was a wealthy hotelier in their hometown of Waterloo, seventy miles from Quebec City. I saw myself as a pretty good match for young Flora & courted her like there was no tomorrow. Now, without going into too much detail, let's just say that we became 'intimate' just a few months into our relationship, she didn't take much enticement I can tell you! Ironically I, the man of failed 'protection' in my previous sexual encounters, threw caution to the wind a couple of times & landed up in the mire again. This time it was with a pregnant Flora, not my plan at all!

Now I am not against children, but at 26 years old they just didn't fit into the foreseeable future, truth be told neither did a wife or any other kind of encumbrance. Nope siree, I just wanted a little fun to fill in the months before my departure to England. So, what to do? I am not a heartless man, I was quite fond of the dear girl but there really was no other solution in my mind than to perform an abortion.

Now I know you're thinking I was a heartless sot, but what alternative did I have without throwing away all those years of hard study? I contemplated my options too, I mean, there were plenty of backstreet clinics who would have obliged in ridding the girl of her little 'obstruction' but hey, why pay good money for a job you can do yourself? Besides, with the Brooks' being such a well-known family, it wouldn't have been long before the gossip-mongers ran forth with their tales.

Flora didn't take too much persuasion after I'd made her see sense, after all I was perfectly able in my capacity of surgeon to carry out the procedure and, if truth be told, her father would have created merry hell with the pair of us had he found out. But sadly find out he did...

The operation went as planned, whereafter I allowed Flora to have a day of bed rest before putting her on the train back home. Little did I know that she always had had a sickly disposition & no sooner had she arrived back in Waterloo, became ill and took to her bed. Apparently, as any concerned parent would do, Mr. Brooks called in a local doctor who soon discovered the girl to be bleeding heavily. Now, as far as I am aware, I performed what I deemed to be a successful clinical process. I can in no way be to blame if my patient is of a slightly delicate constitution. Anyhow, there I was sipping my bourbon in the Ottawa Hotel, blissfully unaware that events were unfolding around me, when Brooks arrived shouting & bawling, and not less importantly waving his shotgun around for all to see. What a commotion that was, embarrassing doesn't even begin to describe it. Being a reasonable man and, if I'm brutally honest, fearing the consequences if I didn't comply, I managed to placate my future father-in-law (yes friend, for that it exactly what he was to become) and followed his entourage to where Flora was waiting at the family residence.

On September 11th 1876 I became a married man for the first and only time in my notorious existence. Now, of course it doesn't end there. Being a very shrewd and calculative suitor, I had already planned my foolproof escape and left the house early the next day while the rest of the household slept on unawares. I hurried forth to my awaiting passenger ship which sailed away at precisely the appointed hour and therefore secured my escape from many years of matrimonial discord.

That wasn't to be the last that I heard from the Brooks family though. After a year of study & familiarizing myself with the seedy underworld of Victorian London, I received a telegram from a mutual acquaintance informing me of poor Flora's passing. Now, you must be getting to know me by now dear buddy, I am certainly not one to pass up an opportunity to make a quick buck, especially given my morphine habit. You see, as the legal spouse of a young lady of means, I felt it my duty to collect what was rightfully mine in inheritance. It would have been a crying shame to leave those funds untouched. I figured I must be due somewhere in the region of $1,000, so I wired Brooks senior outlining my intention to make a claim. All I can say is that he wasn't best pleased to hear from me, but realizing his legal obligation, eventually settled on a payment of $200. All I had to do was sign on the dotted line.

After that escapade I wasn't eager to return to Canada anytime soon, and stayed at St. Thomas's until 1878. Now friend, I don't want to bore you with my endless lists of educational achievements, but you need to know that I am a fully qualified doctor and I have always acted in my patients time of need, albeit not always in their best interests, ha, ha!

Hence my studies progressed at a mediocre pace and I managed to subsidize my flamboyant lifestyle by working as an obstetric clerk. I saw some cases while on duty there I can tell you! This was the first time I had come face-to-face with the 'real' London. I can't say that it changed my feelings towards the city but it did ingrain in me a fascination for the less fortunate souls who passed through those hospital doors.

Some days were so busy that I hardly had time to catch forty-winks, something that I regularly needed to do due to my rather hectic social life. You may expect me to have grown sympathetic towards those unfortunate citizens in my care – the hard-working laborer wringing his hands as he stressed over the birth of his newborn twins, two more mouths to feed in such already difficult times. What about the woman of ill-repute, brought in with complications following her recent pregnancy? Poor wench would either not survive the night or be back on the streets touting for custom within the week. So, call me hard if you must, but instead of feeling an overwhelming urge to care for those wretched people, I felt disgust, animosity and most of all, a growing sense of superiority.

I have to admit that I partied a little too hard sometimes, and was still plagued by the debilitating headaches of previous years. This may have in part caused me to fail my entrance exam to the Royal College of Surgeons, but it certainly didn't hinder my progress. Using my expert knowledge in chloroform, something I had studied with precision and care at McGill, I gained a double first at the Royal College of Physicians and Surgeons in Edinburgh, Scotland.

Edinburgh was, and probably still is, a beautiful and imposing city. My life had begun in the heart of Glasgow but I remembered very little about my Scottish heritage. I felt no connection with those grey and dismal places, how could I, but it was as good a place as any to complete my studies and take those all-important examinations. There were no high-living friends to distract my attention in Edinburgh, although I soon found some fellow students with whom I could discover new antics on my leisure days.

There was a point when I seriously considered giving up on completing my degree. I wasn't even sure that the institutes in Canada would check to see if my certificates were genuine. I think my conscience and duty to my father won out, as I buckled down until the final tests were over. My friend, I can honestly tell you that during those long nights of study, my mind always wandered back to London. It was, without doubt, the most unique place that I had ever had the pleasure of visiting. I belonged amongst those lodging houses in Lambeth, I reveled in the drunken scenes outside taverns and I just couldn't quell my thirst for watching those dirty whores trade their bodies for coins.

Anyhow, once my qualifications were stamped and sealed, I had to decide where my fate lay. Not for one moment did I contemplate seeking employment in Scotland. There was something slightly depressing about the high granite walls that circuited the city of Edinburgh and I knew that I could only be truly happy in the midst of chaos and crime.

And so it came to pass that, with the certificates safely encased in my leather-bound luggage, I now headed back across the Atlantic to embark on my newly-qualified life as an abortionist & expert in all matters chemical.

Bear with me dear reader, now the tale really begins…

3

Hiscock's Buildings, Dundas Street, London, Ontario

So, here I am, back in Canada with my whole career before me.

I had learned a lot in London, a city where every man could immerse himself in both the professional and pleasurable spoils of life. I could easily have stayed but being closer to my family was like having a financial safety net and I wasn't quite ready to give it up just yet. I still kept in touch with some of the old boys from St. Thomas's, in particular those who had a penchant for the dark side, who knew when I might need a friend?

My second reason for departing those English shores was personal. Now I'm no casanova, but it seemed to me that the London ladies just couldn't keep their eyes or hands off of me. I cut a dashing figure in my sleek Canadian finery and my smooth transatlantic accent sure didn't hinder my female conquests. There were the ladies in the West End with their private carriages and healthy bank balances tucked away in Threadneedle Street. Then there were the filthy harlots who walked the streets around my lodgings in Lambeth. Sometimes all a fellow wanted or needed was a quick ride without the courtship and those wanton sluts sure knew how to handle their punters. I spent many a night in the company of my friend 'R' and his group of city heiresses, only to wander back along Westminster Bridge in search of a 'quick release'. So dear friend, you might wonder what was wrong? Why leave such an agreeable situation?

I can best describe it as physical boredom. I mean, imagine if you found that you had a fondness for French cheese, just couldn't get enough of that creamy texture and pale smooth skin, but now envisage eating that same cheese for every meal of every day. Tell me reader, how long would it take before you heaved and retched at the very sight of your beloved fromage? Not too long I can bet. Now sure, you could always try a different cheese, something with a sharper taste or more pungent odour, but after all is said and done, it would still be cheese.

Incidentally, my headaches had worsened to a thundering roar, which at times left me shut up in my rooms for days. It would be easier to obtain larger quantities of morphine across the Atlantic, London was such a small place with every pharmacist asking questions & measuring every petty dose so very carefully. Yes, I definitely needed to leave.

And so, despite my very pleasurable existence, I bid farewell to 'R' (for that is how best to refer to him at this point, at least until I know you better dear reader) and left him with a few of my personal effects, promising that I would indeed be back in the not too distant future.

Of course, being such excellent chums, I told my dear 'R' that should any of my belongings be of use to him, he was more than welcome to avail himself. Being a student, I had nothing of great value but was more than happy to oblige when 'R' explained that he had taken rather a shine to my tie pin. Now reader, that was my horseshoe tie pin which was to feature quite prominently in a different decade, in a very notorious set of circumstances. I must admit that I was quite fond of that particular piece of jewellery, and even had in my possession a professional photograph of myself wearing it. But, as I told you, my good friend 'R' thought it would add sophistication to his attire, so I was more than willing to make it a parting gift.

My other belongings included medical books, several items of clothing and some rather exotic pictures. Well, I call those photographs 'exotic' but to be frank with you, they were pretty 'erotic' actually.

I had for some time been collecting what some gents referred to as 'unsavory' poses of women in all manner of undress. I am certainly no pervert, dear reader, but one can't help but develop a passion for these things. To look upon a naked woman can help a man to become aroused when he doesn't have the fortune to find himself in a position to partake of such delights. Of course, some of my companions found my desires quite unacceptable, but 'R', he understood.

Anyway, it was time to start forging a profitable career for myself, therefore now you find me departed and safely back in Canada.

I created a neat little set up for myself in Dundas Street, private rooms befitting for a gent, together with an outer room which I could use to see my patients. Hence Dr.Cream's Clinic for Women was founded, not the first of its kind but one which made me a handsome profit for very little physical exertion. I spent several days getting everything ship-shape and ready for business before opening my doors. It wasn't long before the ladies came scurrying in, with sidelong sheepish glances, wringing their hands in anxiety.

Now folks, you must know by now what I mean by a 'Women's Clinic'. I provided a service for those unmarried young things who had given in to their lustful beaus and carried the seed to prove it. So you see, it was Doctor Cream who helped them out of their unfortunate state, with tea and sympathy and a quick operation to boot. Now you might wonder how I could make a healthy living out of abortions alone, but believe me, there was no shortage of visitors, especially as I was new to the area and could be trusted to keep my mouth firmly closed.

As this was to be my first real business, I made every attempt to give the clinic a professional but relaxed atmosphere. I had limited funds with which to furnish the rooms, but feel that my efforts were more than adequate considering the lower-class of clientele that I aimed to attract.

I employed the services of a char-woman for the first few days of my residence and gave instructions on how I expected the window-panes to gleam and the floor rugs to be dust-free. All in all, the end result was one of a homely environment, one where my patients would feel relaxed enough to part with their hard-earned cash.

Never in my career have I doubted my abilities, whether it be medical, professional or personal. Dundas Street was the first rung on a high ladder for me, it would create the much needed financial incentive to move on to greater things but would also prove to my father that he had made a good investment when funding my college tuition.

Being in Ontario, on the other hand, would mean I was close enough to home for my family to stay in contact, but far enough away for me to have personal freedom. You understand me don't you friend? There are times when a gent needs space to discover his passions and iron out his short-comings. Not that I had any yet, ha ha!

Everything went along according to plan for a few months before disaster struck. You know, I'm sure these unlucky bitches follow me around like flies attracted to a cow pat! I mean, every time my life is thrown into turmoil there's a woman behind it. Anyhow, life had been sweet, I was getting some funds together and met a few pretty faces along the way, when one sunny afternoon a young chambermaid graced my office with her presence.

Katherine Hutchinson Gardener, or 'Kate' as she liked to be referred to, had gotten herself into the same predicament as the many young girls who had sat on my couch before her. She told me she was nineteen years old, and I'm guessing she hadn't lied about that. I sat there and listened as she poured out the whole sorry story of how she had been seduced by a young courier from a few miles out of town, and how he'd swiftly disappeared after hearing from Kate how her 'monthly courses' had stopped suddenly. Even to a girl of nineteen it hadn't taken much figuring out to realize that she was with child and very much on her own. So there I sat tolerating her sniveling and silently wondering how I was going to drop the subject of payment into this now very one-sided conversation.

I won't burden you with the loathsome details, but it came to pass that little Miss Kate didn't have the means to pay for her impending treatment. Now that should have been the end of it, close the door, goodbye, try a cheaper doctor etc, but something inside me just snapped that afternoon. I don't know if it was due to the terrible headache I had looming over me that day, or just pure frustration at having had to sit through her whole sorry narrative, but I let loose like an arrow from a bow.

At first it was just about calming her down, stopping the sobs while at the same time explaining that I ran a business, not a charity, so a little dose of chloroform on my handkerchief sufficed. Then heck, the darn silly bitch started struggling and I was forced to press harder with my hand across her mouth. I don't rightly remember too much after that, I vaguely recall getting her to the outhouse and leaving her there to regain consciousness. What I can say in all honesty is that whether she awoke or not I really didn't give a damn. I had other patients to see and I had money to make.

Well, business was interrupted the very next day when a couple of detectives from Ontario showed up. Somebody had stumbled across Miss. Gardener's body.

I pride myself on how calm I managed to be during those initial questionings. I freely admitted that the girl had been to see me, but ardently denied giving her treatment on ethical grounds. I just wasn't that kind of doctor! I even gave them a subtle hint that she was distressed and may have taken a bottle of chloroform from my dispensary while I was out of the room, her chosen way out of a lamentable situation. I implored them to be reasonable, how could this despicable episode be connected to me?

Anyhow, the following two weeks passed without incident & despite further interrogation, they didn't arrest me. I mean, how could they? Where was the evidence?

The County Coroner concluded that suicide was impossible, well I guess that was a little far-fetched, but instead returned a verdict of 'Death from chloroform administered by an unknown person'. I was in the clear.

Now friend, you may think that I had a lucky escape there, but that stupid mistake cost me my business. The local press named my clinic, and me, causing patients to seek treatment elsewhere in the town. This was certainly one time where I didn't revel in the publicity surrounding me. I couldn't survive on fresh air alone, and although I had managed to save a good sum it wouldn't support me indefinitely.

I even found that seeking solitude in local bars provoked idle gossip & snide titters behind my back. Now, if a man can't find tranquility in the bottom of his bourbon glass, he's in the wrong town, so once again I found myself seeking pastures new. This time I would cross the border into the U.S.A. where Dr. Cream was an unknown entity and I could mingle quietly in the crowd. Or, at least, I believed it so.

Now reader, you must be thinking that I have no trouble constantly reinventing myself, moving silently around like a dark shadow on a sunny afternoon, is that what you think?

Well, let me assure you, that life was always a sure thing for me, I believed I had the luck of the Devil, or some dirty dark angel whispering in my ear. It was one or the other that gave me the assured ability of being able to talk myself out of difficulty and move on without hindrance. Someone was looking down on me, and I was going to grab their helping hand with full force.

Dear friend, will you now come with me on my next adventure, to territories unknown and fields of gold? You might learn a little more about me along the way. Stop and think friend, does that frighten or excite you?

Carry on this journey with me, if you dare…

4

434, West Madison Street, Chicago

Hello Friend, so you decided to travel with me to the next city did you? Don't know whether you are brave, curious or simply foolish but I guess time will tell.

So now you find me in Chicago in August 1879, amidst the chaos & hubbub of a bustling metropolis. I had landed on my feet again & found rooms with a suitable area to set up a new clinic in a bustling area of the city, which just happened to be close to the red-light district, giving me a plentiful supply of customers. Of course my line of business was to be the same as previously, I mean if you're good at a job why change your profession?

My new landlady, Mrs. Gridley, was a very agreeable type and we got along just fine. She had exceptionally good female intuition & seemed to know when a helping hand would be appreciated, but in the same thread, she instinctively knew when to discreetly disappear. Hence, I quickly settled in to my new neighbourhood, even meeting some very respectable families on the social circuit, some of whom were to become part of my undoing in the future...

Now you may be thinking that by setting up another clinic I hadn't learned any lessons from the past. But, dear reader, you would be wrong to presume so. I was very careful not to perform the 'intimate' kind of operations on my premises & learned quickly how to cover my tracks.

It seemed a perfectly normal practice for other doctors in the area to employ a midwife to assist with these procedures, in that the woman would rent a room for the purpose of clinical use by the doctor and then stay present after the abortion to clean up the patient and then send them on their way. This arrangement suited me well, and there was certainly no shortage of midwives willing to earn a few dollars in exchange for a couple of hours drudgery.

And so, business progressed. The tenement buildings that lined the local streets provided two things, lodgings for dozens of prostitutes and a steady stream of customers requiring doctors like me to terminate their unwanted pregnancies. By the time I reached Chicago, I had my relentless headaches back under control with my own concoction of morphine, strychnine & cocaine. A little of each seemed to keep my head balanced & even gave me a little boost as an aphrodisiac, although by now I was beginning to sicken of street-walkers and feared that I may succumb to further infection should I partake of their wares.

In fact, my feelings became so profound, that I promised myself only to be sexually active with respectable ladies, should they allow me to have the honour, ha, ha...

That Winter in Chicago was a cold and thankless one, the streets were quieter and so was my clinic. However, it gave me considerably more time to enjoy my social circle, especially with my new found friends, the McClelland family who kindly invited me to spend the festive season at their home.

They had some wonderful folks keeping house nearby, the lovely Eva Adams being a particular favorite of mine. How I've lost count of all those nights when I played the piano while she sang such melodious festive carols. Eva was a fine lady but too mature in years for us to have a romantic connection. Instead we took to debating for hours about elections and local government candidates until finally the wine bottle was empty and we held our sides with laughter.

The McClelland's were honest, church-going people and I feel that they took me under their wing out of compassion, for I was new to the city, and my social circle small. There were many gatherings that Christmas and I clearly remember Mrs. McClelland pushing this young lady and that forward to have an introduction to me. I was sorely tempted friend, to look past the faults of those curvy young females who tried so desperately to catch my eye. Call me particular if you wish, but there was always some reason for me not to pursue them.

Perhaps it was their unexciting conversation or lack of worldly knowledge but I was seldom aroused. I knew that I was a good catch and wholly deserved a wit to match my own, a strong sensuous woman who would not be alarmed by my expectations in our bed-chamber. In that circle of friends, at that time, I knew that no such female could be found.

As seems to be the pattern with my life, when things are running smoothly, something will happen to blot my diary. And happen it did, in February 1880, just six weeks after I had enjoyed partaking of fine wine and roasted goose with my distinguished hosts.

My day had been none too extraordinary, in fact a little mundane if truth be told, when I was sent a message from Hattie Mack, a Negro woman that I regularly hired to be present during my operations. Mrs. Mack had sent word that she had a customer for me & was waiting at a lodging house nearby. I was with a patient when the message arrived, so it was a good thirty minutes before I gathered my medical bag, donned my cape and muffler, then set off to perform what should have been a routine procedure.

It only took me fifteen minutes or so to arrive at the shabby apartment building & on knocking at the door I was ushered upstairs to where Hattie Mack was waiting with a rather pale, skinny young girl lying on the divan in a greying nightgown, which I could clearly see had blood spattered on the front. It seemed that Mrs. Mack had been impatient and had already started the procedure to remove the foetus on her own. I cursed the black woman and began a clean-up operation, scraping the girl's womb and removing the remaining clots. I then instructed Mrs. Mack to finish up while I hastily retreated back through the biting wind to the warmth of my rooms. That should have been an end to it, but as with that incident in Dundas Street, the next morning my coffee and newspaper were interrupted by the city police hammering at my door.

At first, when they asked me about Mary Anne Faulkner, I was at a loss as to whom they were referring. After all, I hadn't been introduced to the waif-like harlot awaiting my services. It was only after telling me that they already had Hattie Mack in custody for the prostitute's death that it dawned on me what had happened. Nevertheless, I too was arrested and spent a harrowing two nights in a cold, damp cell before being hauled up in front of a jury. My lawyer, a trusted friend, played his part well and despite the charges of manslaughter, he managed to convince the twelve gents on the bench that I was merely present to try to save the young woman after the bungled abortion by an unqualified midwife. Poor Doctor Cream, just giving a helping hand and unjustly prosecuted, life was so unfair! Inevitably I walked free that day, back to my clinic to salvage my reputation.

Several uneventful months followed, well dear reader at least I mean months that had no disastrous conclusions. As a result of more media attention following the Faulkner girl's death, I had decided to take an alternative medical path and spent my time preparing various remedies to market in good faith. Whether they actually worked or not was for my takers to decide, but for the most part they certainly did no harm. Oh dear, you see there I go again, I have spoken too soon.

My ingenious morning-after pills were the most popular of my medications, can you imagine such a wonderful invention in the late nineteenth century? I had dozens of takers, but was always careful to simply send them to the pharmacy with a prescription, I had neither the intention or necessity to get tied up in the preparation of such drugs. After all, if something were to go wrong, would that not put the blame on to the chemist and not the doctor?

Each pill was laced with strychnine, a poison which, with the correct dosage, would induce a miscarriage, the purpose for which I had intended them. Now, friend, it must be noted that the measures of strychnine must be exact in order to serve the prescription correctly, therefore too little would have no more serious effect than stomach cramps but too much would cause agonizing seizures, followed by death.

I do not know if I gave the correct dosage to Ellen Stack. She died shortly after taking her morning-after pills, and my clinic was once again at the center of a murder investigation.

I was convinced that I had done no wrong this time and, determined to clear my name, I wrote several letters to Frank Pyatt the chemist warning him that he should come clean and admit that he had made a mistake when putting up Miss Stack's medicine. Of course, old Pyatt was quite irate and denied any knowledge of wrong-doing. Our verbal battle became quite heated and before long both Pyatt and I were arrested. Of course, I wasn't unduly worried, there was little evidence against me and within a few days we both walked free.

That was by no means the end of the matter, and quite an investigation was launched, but try as they might there was no way to directly link the blame to either Pyatt or myself.

I felt free to continue my business now, but fretted that in due course my carelessness would lead to a capture where liberty would not be found so easily. I cursed myself, sometimes I was a damned idiot, taking risks when all I really should be doing was keeping my head low and making a decent living. I was still young, but my incessant recklessness would be my undoing if I wasn't careful, I needed to think. How could I keep my business afloat in Chicago? Another move just wasn't viable at that time. I pondered long and hard, until soon, the answer came.

I figured that if the use of opiates were helping me to control my vile disease, why couldn't they be used to treat patients with previously incurable conditions? Take epilepsy for example, surely a few drops of strychnine, mixed with some laudanum could have a profound effect on a fellow with uncontrollable tremors. It was certainly worth a shot, and thank the Lord it worked.

Before long, I had formulated the perfect dosage of each drug and Dr. Cream's remedy for epilepsy was born. There were folks who called me a 'Quack' but the constant line of customers queueing for my vile-tasting elixir soon outnumbered the sceptics. If I may be so bold as to say, my creation worked for those who believed in it and business was soon at its peak again.

Mrs. Gridley became of great assistance during those busy days, offering tea to those who sought my aid and putting out extra seats in her own hallway to create a waiting room of sorts.

I was once again in fine form, having found my niche if you like. I could once again afford to have my suits cut at the very best drapers shop and to dine at the trendiest places in town. Life was swell, and this time I intended to be very careful to keep it that way. I befriended local businessmen whom I deemed useful in conducting future affairs. Amongst my closest allies were pharmacists, printers and senior doctors, who could be relied upon for last minute medical supplies, advertising leaflets and death certificates. Oh, friend, that last one just popped up there by default, there were few deaths but it was always useful to have a professional on hand.

Throughout my childhood I had possessed a wild determination to succeed and it was no less apparent n my business negotiations. I knew that I had a natural aptitude for dealing with people's medical needs and in my era there were few doctors who chose to delve in to the seedier complications born from lust and destitution. This is where I believed I could make a real difference. I could help to eradicate such foul diseases as that which held my very own sanity hostage and cleanse the community by aiding those pitiful whores to rid themselves of their unwanted bastards.

I know what you think of me, dear reader, but had you lived your days crossing the street to avoid drunken brawls and hollering prostitutes, you would reward my valiant effort. Every city across America, Canada and Europe was in the grip of a dirty secret. Only very close inspection could reveal the gravity of its seedy underworld, like a Pandora's box filled with disease, insanity and filth.

In the past I supposed I had been young and naive, but now Thomas Neill Cream was growing up, I was taking stock of my life and independently making a decent living.

I wrote home to my father several times, letting him know that I was doing well in the profession to which he had steered me, but in the meantime hoping too that the newspaper reports of the previous year had made no impact over the border. I also wrote to 'R' in London and received several letters in response. It seemed he too had been having quite a time, even taking risks of his own with the law. He urged me to visit England again, but I had promised myself that the next time I walked Queen Victoria's streets it would be as a man of independent means. Besides, I was sure that 'R' didn't need my help with his escapades, if our days at St. Thomas's had been anything to go by 'R' could actually teach me a thing or two.

And so dear reader, I leave you to your imagination now. You have seen me at my worst (or is there more?) and you now know me to have enjoyed moderate success. It would be easy to leave my tale there, but unfortunately there is so very much more to tell you. Be prepared for the hair to rise on your neck friend, for my evil has only just begun.

5

Chicago, continued

Are you surprised dear friend? That I am still here in West Madison Street? Still doing a good trade in epilepsy tonic & none the worse for my little brush with the law? Have faith in me, I am one of life's survivors, I will always be lurking not far from your door, peering over your shoulder or guiding you down the path to the dark side. Ha, Ha, after all, I remain here to tell you of my deeds do I not? Anyhow, friend, I guess you'll want to know what happened next. Bet you're wondering how many sweet young maidens succumbed to my devilish charms, followed by the permanent sleep of a premature death. Well, none is the answer, at least not for a while. Let me explain…

Business was at its very best. My epilepsy remedy had saved my skin and some evenings I lay exhausted in front of a roaring fire after a constant stream of customers had bustled in begging me to write up a prescription for 'the cure'. Yes, they were good days, profitable and satisfying. Now, you know me of old dear friend don't you? No scene would be complete without a female or two to keep me company. It just so happens that there were a couple of young ladies who captured my interest, but this time I was very cautious not to let them manipulate me. Most importantly, I had to be discreet, didn't want them scratching the surface of my true personality, and certainly didn't want to risk those divine cherubs learning about each other!

The first lady to come to my attention was by pure chance, a slender woman in her early thirties who had an air of superiority about her, not someone to suffer fools gladly. However, the defining attraction of Julia Stott was the fact that she was married. Now, I know what's rattling through that confused mind of yours, how could I dare to involve myself with an already taken female? It seemed to me that there would be less romantic complication & less likelihood that she would want to sink her talons into my healthy bank balance, and by all accounts it was quite easy, a little subtle persuasion by turning on my charismatic charms and that particular forbidden fruit was ripe for the picking.

Now, Mrs. Stott's husband was a faithful customer of mine, a railroad agent by the name of Daniel, who suffered dreadful bouts of epileptic fits but had become convinced that my tonic was serving its purpose in controlling his seizures. However, being a man of sixty plus years and not in an ideal physical condition, Daniel Stott had no desire to take the arduous train journey from his home in Garden Prairie, Boone County to the dusty streets of Chicago.

Hence, that is where Julia entered the scene. Stott's pretty, much younger wife, was only too happy to travel across state to the bustling city. Not only could she collect her husband's prescription from the hands of his handsome young doctor (and that would be me dear reader, in case you forgot) but Mrs. Stott could also avail herself of the shopping district, a worthwhile compensation for her overnight stay. Before you start jumping to conclusions, I will vehemently deny that Julia Stott was ever a guest in my bed-chamber. Oh no, I was very careful there and ensured that I secured her a room with Mrs. Gridley on each and every visit. (What I won't deny is turning my clinic sign to 'CLOSED' every once in a while to partake in the 'joys of the flesh' so to speak – but don't frown dear friend, that betrothed strumpet enjoyed herself fully in my amorous clutches).

And so, the months passed and our impetuous liaison continued. Daniel Stott's prescription required filling more frequently of course, but there were still weeks between visits when I found myself in pursuit of alternative entertainment. This is where Mrs. McClelland once again found me on her doorstep seeking intellectual conversation and a mutual appreciation of music. It also did no harm to my reputation as eligible bachelor that Mrs. McClelland had an attractive, daughter of some twenty-eight years, who was only too happy to avail herself of Dr. Cream's attention.

Now I wouldn't call the McClelland's daughter dull, but she certainly lacked the social skills of a city hostess. Sometimes I found myself recounting the same tale twice for lack of interaction on her part. Oh, the young lady was pleasant enough but twenty-eight years of living in her mother's shadow had done little to broaden her horizons. There was very little physical attraction towards her, on my part anyway, but Mrs. McClelland would always insist I sat opposite her daughter at dinner and would give knowing winks should we happen to catch each other's eye.

Given a choice between Julia Stott and the McClelland girl I would almost certainly chose the former. Julia was experienced and feisty, just the antidote for a long cold winter spent sleeping alone.

However, Mrs. McClelland had no knowledge of my personal affairs and, to her, Julia Stott was quite simply a dutiful wife come to the city to collect her husband's prescription. And so, the months passed, with every Christian date being met with an invitation to dinner and every acceptance being tinged with an ounce of guilt on my part. In hindsight, I can see how a betrothal of marriage into the McClelland family might have saved me from the years of misery that would follow. But, who are we to foretell the future friend, a marriage then might have brought me to an early grave.

Perhaps I was blinded by lust, or simply felt myself smarter than the average Casanova, but it never occurred to me that I would need to make choices, decisions that would impact my future and eventually my sanity.

When Julia Stott first hinted to me that she thought it was time to increase her husband's dosage, I merely took it in jest, something said on a whim but not to be heeded too earnestly. But gradually the innuendos became less tactful and she began to unravel her plans. As a widow, rid of her over-bearing grizzled spouse, Julia would be free to enjoy life again and imparted to me her wish to share her spoils with the benevolent Thomas Cream. Heck, what was a guy to do? Murdering a full-blooded male was a whole different scenario to those skirmishes of my past. I figured I could help, as long as it was financially rewarding, but the fatal dose had to be administered by Mr. Stott's doting wife. I really should have heard those instinctive alarm bells inside my head, telling me to back away, but the imminent sound of rustling banknotes was just too tempting and a seemingly foolproof plan was devised.

On Saturday 11th June 1881, Julia arrived at my office around eleven to collect the very last prescription for her elderly husband. I was busy with another patient and sent her away to get lunch. When Julia returned at 3pm, she seemed pensive, which I guess was understandable given what she intended to do on her return home the following day, but I simply felt irritable as I wanted neither her tears nor her questions that afternoon. She wanted to know if it would be quick, the death I mean, but what did she expect? A blow by blow account of the poor man's suffering to come? I reminded her again that I would write the prescription but whether she administered the drugs or not was to be her choice, and hers alone. I feared that the woman was disillusioned about our relationship and fretted that she may expect a more permanent commitment from me once her husband was six feet under. Regardless, there was always Canada. I could escape to the north if need be, my father would be only too glad to welcome his prodigal son back to the fold.

With only momentary hesitation, I scribbled on my clinical notepad and ushered Julia Stott out of the door. As I knew she also intended to get her teeth done at Dr. Day's, over the river, it would surely be a while until she returned. That was some small blessing at least, I figured that the further she had to walk, the more time I would have alone to think, make my plans and ultimately free myself from any undue romantic implications. Later that afternoon, the soon-to-be widow returned and showed me the drugs that she had fetched. I checked the contents, divided between a few sugar and calamine capsules in order that the bitter taste of strychnine be concealed on digestion, and felt confident that all was in order. It was late by this time and I was obliged to procure a room from Mrs. Gridley so that Julia may rest her head in Chicago for one final night.

The next morning, as the train for Boone County pulled out of the sidings, I exhaled deeply. Soon I would be a little richer, and then time to put a stop to this whole affair.

That evening I dined on steak at a fine local establishment and then called upon my friends the McClelland's, only to find that they were being entertained by a clairvoyant of some dubious repute. I could see that my venerable hosts were taken in completely by the psychic's trickery but was dumbfounded to be on the receiving end of her predictions.

It was a ridiculous scenario from the start. Every person present was instructed to be seated at the dining table and hold hands in a circle. The lanterns were then dimmed so low that one could barely make out the silhouettes of those awaiting instruction.

For the first couple of 'readings' I bowed out, insisting that I would gain far more pleasure from watching than I ever could from taking part. So, as it was, instead of taking a chair amongst the group, I poured myself a glass of claret and looked on from the comfort of the piano stool.

All manner of premonitions were forthcoming that evening and the party gasped in awe as that charlatan of a fortuneteller reeled off one personal prediction after another. I was thankful to have joined when the session was already in full swing. It was tedious to hear how "Mrs. McClelland would be suffering from arthritis next winter" (did she not always have aching joints being nearly sixty years of age?) and how her handsome son would find himself a bride within the year (surely that had been a topic of conversation spanning weeks).

Anyway, dear reader, I ducked out of their pathetic charade as long as was politely possible and then, amidst cheers and cajoling, took my seat at the table between Mrs. McClelland and that fraudster clairvoyant. "A patient of yours will die tonight' she foretold, amidst the group of onlookers who glanced at me to gage my reaction. Of course, I brushed it off as pure hogwash, but it sure put the dampeners on my appetite for socializing and I couldn't wait to make my excuses and leave.

A sleepless night followed, my head pounding as I mulled over the implications of my tryst with Julia Stott. A slight part of me wanted to believe that she would carry out the plan, pay me my dues and then give me a motive to dispose of her in the same way she had so heartlessly wanted to rid herself of her husband. Of course, no such fortune was to befall me that summer. Instead a disaster loomed on the horizon, one which would see me gasping in indignation. Dear reader, continue, and please help me. Assist me in understanding how a man of my intelligence can have been so witless.

The next morning I received a telegram, simply telling me that my patient, Daniel Stott, was dead. It seemed the poor fellow had suffered an epileptic seizure severe enough to finish him off. Relieved, but perplexed, I waited.

For two days, nothing came. No message from that femme fatale, but more importantly no money either. A seed of doubt entered my mind, had Mrs. Stott out-witted me? Had she planned to play the rich grieving widow all along?

What to do? Bide my time? Nope, that really wasn't my style. I threw caution to the wind that night and sent a telegram to the Boone County Coroner, aiming to point the finger of blame at the rightful culprit. It read: 'SUSPECT FOUL PLAY. WILL WRITE IMMEDIATELY. DR. CREAM'. I followed this with an explanation in which I accused the pharmacist of making a mistake when preparing the prescription, but in the same note hinted that Mrs. Stott may have been to blame whilst administering the medication. If I wasn't to benefit from my part in all this, then Julia Stott should be thrown to the wolves, taking the damn chemist with her.

Much to my dismay, the Coroner paid no heed to my letter, putting it down to be a fanciful prank no less. Therefore my hand was forced and I put pen to paper once again, this time to the District Attorney who took the matter into his own hands. Soon afterwards, the body of Daniel Stott was exhumed, revealing a large quantity of strychnine in his stomach. At last, the authorities had listened to me.

Feeling avenged, I quickly boarded a train for Canada and alighted in Windsor, Ontario. It felt good to have my feet back on familiar soil, there was something comforting in returning to the land of my youth. I booked in to a very comfortable hotel and prepared to avail myself of the local attractions until the distasteful mess in Illinois had blown over.

Sometimes I look back and feel that I must have had a premonition about my impending arrest, as my days of freedom up there in Windsor were filled with trepidation and ceaseless nightmares. You see, it was just a matter of days until they found me. Julia Stott, the bitch, had turned state's evidence and pinned the whole damned homicide on me.

Returning to the States unleashed in me a wrath, the likes of which I had never known before but was to learn to live with for the rest of my days. As constables escorted me to Boone County Jail, I was shown no mercy. No time to gather my books or collect my warmest undergarments. A cloud of the darkest grey had gathered above me, this time there was to be no reprieve. There was no-one to administer the drugs that my brain so desperately craved, leaving me mentally tortured until the trial began.

6

Boone County Jail, Illinois

It was a hot summer that year, the air was dry, the wind only gathering momentum once the sun had gone down, and I clearly remember my first few days in Boone County Jail as being quite tedious, stiflingly warm and fraught with boredom. I at least managed to get some sleep whilst I waited for my lawyer to arrive. Little did I realize that dreams were to be something of the past once the trial had begun. Of course, initially I really believed that in just a few days I would be free. I mean, how could the finger of blame be pointed at me? This was all a misunderstanding, they had the wrong person in custody and as soon as Julia Stott did the decent thing and confessed, I would be at liberty to go back to my thriving business.

I fully expected my captors to treat me with respect and leniency but it hardly seemed to matter to the Sheriff that I had prominence in the community. This was a small locality compared to the humdrum of Chicago. He couldn't see past the crime. A well-respected local man had been murdered and, as far as the Sheriff was concerned, the assailant was now on vacation in Boone County Jail.

For three full days I was blissfully unaware that both Julia Stott and I were to stand trial for the murder of her husband, fully expecting this to be an instance of my wrongful arrest. I was ignorant too that it would take over three months of court appearances before the Judge would come to his final verdict. I always considered myself to be a strong-minded individual whose resolve could not be easily broken, but upon the arrival of the venerable Chas Fuller, my attorney, I quickly realized that unlike my previous brush with the law, this was a far more serious case. Looking back, I see how flippant I was at first, knowing that I was implicated in a patient's death was serious enough but I had confidence that justice would be served and I would walk free. Of course, I have spent my lifetime being a rascal but this time I really was innocent, set up by a scorned bitch, who really just couldn't bring herself to share me. Shame on her!

Well, anyhow, I will try to describe to you those long arduous days in the courthouse, then perhaps you will sympathize with me my friend. I had but one good suit of clothes with which to present myself, and felt the eyes of the town upon my shabby appearance as I was ushered on to the bench every day. It was most interesting to see how my so-called friends had plenty to say in matters which little concerned them. The first to take the stand on oath was Mrs. Mary McClelland. What a turn-coat ! I listened intently as the lady who had poured me wine at Thanksgiving and showered me with gifts at Christmas told lie after lie while avoiding my gaze at all costs. Apparently Mrs. McClelland recalled a conversation in which I had told her of Daniel Stott's impending death and then supposedly implicated myself as the 'other man' who had his eye on Stott's beautiful young wife. She also described how I had tried to seduce her lovely daughter Lena whilst planning to poison Mrs. McClelland and her son. Really? Dear Lady, why on earth did you bid me over the thresh-hold of your home if you feared such evil may come to pass? Later, my true advocates, Mr. and Mrs. Martin and the lovely hostess Eva Adams, testified that no such conversation had taken place, but I fear that the seeds of doubt had already been sown in the minds of those who mattered.

Day after day I was taken from my cell to the courthouse, amidst jeering from the waiting public. That didn't bother me so much really. It was the three hour wait between breakfast and the arrival of my attorney that began to take its toll.

I have always been a man who needs to be occupied in some task or other, be it reading, taking in the city theatre shows or concocting a new potion for my patients. But there, in that jail, the only thoughts that could fill my dreary hours were those that might possibly release me from this abominable situation.

My mind churned over the dozens of conversations that had passed between myself and Julia Stott. Surely there must be something that could be used to her detriment? Alas, I could think of no note sent by that woman to my office, no declaration which may support my case in her infatuation with me, and no telegram cursing her husband. Julia had been so very careful. Had she really planned it this way all along? For all I know, I might have been just one pawn in her string of illicit affairs. After all, she had been more than willing to satisfy my sexual cravings, I would even go so far as to suggest that she instigated our liaisons on more than one occasion. Calculating bitch!

About five weeks in to the trial, I returned to my cell to find it occupied by a rather scrawny looking chap wearing breeches and suspenders but no shirt. I can't for the life of me remember his name, but our conversations will haunt me forever. This fellow was a common thief, serving a short term for breaking and entering the home of a local merchant. I remember thinking at the time that any dialogue entered into with this man would be entirely therapeutic, chatter to pass the interminable hours inside. He was nobody, just a larcenist doing his servitude, right? Wrong! I never imagined it within the bounds of possibility that this cad would end up in court, at my trial, giving evidence for the prosecution. What a dirty trick, thinking that he could beseech himself a shorter sentence in return for dishing the dirt on my 'supposed' involvement with Daniel Stott's poisoning. For one whole afternoon he recanted how I had confessed to plotting the homicide whilst Mrs. Stott was totally unaware.

I had learned a valuable lesson, and from that day forward vowed to never let another human being within an inch of my confidence.

In between grueling sessions in court, I was provided with paper and pen in order to make notes. Even though I had full faith in Chas

Fuller, and counted on him to represent me well, I wanted to ensure that every avenue of my innocence had been explored, with every possible witness subpoenaed to say their piece in my favor. Unfortunately, the prosecution seemed well-versed in Julia Stott's story and did their very best to paint me in the blackest hues, twisting every alibi and conversation to suit their own ends.

Dear Reader, I am sure you can see that it is very hard to be represented against a murder charge when you are fully aware that there were only two witnesses to the full scenario of events that took place. One was of course myself, and the other was that vengeful woman who had fear running through her vindictive veins. I knew that rather than risk being implicated, Julia Stott would go to any lengths to pin the blame on me but right up until the very end I truly hoped that her conscience would get the better of her and she would confess all. How wrong I was.

Slowly the weeks turned in to months and I still felt no closer to gaining my freedom. Nights were spent pacing my damp and dreary cell, while weekends were spent writing letters to those whom I hoped may be able to testify in my favor. I even wrote to Mrs. McClelland in the hope that she would realize the anxiety she had caused me in using her idle gossip as a deposition, but the papers came back with seals unbroken. I was finally starting to crumble.

By the time Julia Stott was called to the stand I knew that there was little left for me to do but hope that her heart would save me. However, I was unprepared for her perfect performance as grieving widow, with fluttering lashes and downcast eyes. That woman was born to take the stage. Keeping her voice barely above a whisper as she carefully maneuvered the prosecutions' probing questions, it would have been entirely appropriate to stand up and give a round of applause. Bravo Julia, what a splendid exhibition!

Without actually seeing Julia Stott groomed for court it may well be hard for you to imagine just what a beautiful and demure creature she was to those who looked on in earnest from the galleries. Of course the bitch avoided eye contact with me at all costs. I felt the heat searing through her as I constantly tried to get her to glance in my direction, but that woman was well-trained, she was taking no chances. It took no time at all for any doubters to see that poor Mrs. Stott had been duped by her husband's physician.

I felt no love, passion or desire for Julia Stott as she stood there testifying against me. Every ounce of compassion for her ebbed away with every breath she took. Each day of each week left me more and more infuriated at how she had managed to emerge from this whole affair smelling of roses, whilst I, quite literally, smelled worse than a street hound.

Of course, being a concerned ally, you must be wondering how I fared mentally during the trial. I have to confess that I was lucid and coherent throughout, but thankful to Mr. Fuller who brought the necessary medication to keep me on a durable track. I had no desire to divulge the dirty details of my affliction but instead allowed the authorities to think that I was cursed with migraines and night terrors.

It bothered me gravely that my semblance suffered. A man who had always had a penchant for the luxuries afforded to those who moved in high circles, I no longer looked the well-groomed young city doctor with life at his fingertips. My shirt cuffs were beginning to fray and my whiskers were increasingly unkempt. I needed a hot bath and a bucketful of cologne, but that was the least of my worries. It is only natural that a fellow would lose his self-esteem in such a place as Boone County Jail, but I lost more than that, I lost my dignity.

When retribution came, it was brutal and swift. Only I was to be incarcerated while the tempestuous whore walked away scot free, the only damage done, her reputation a little jaded. I hardly comprehended the words of the judge as he sealed my fate, I heard 'Term of your natural life' and nothing more. According to Chas Fuller, I surged forward and swept every last document from the table as my temper raged. This just wasn't happening. How could it be? This time I was innocent, my only sin was one of sub-consciously nurturing the evil mind of my lover. The minutes that followed were such that I felt cocooned in a huge bubble. Voices took on a slow and retarded pace, faces became distorted and blurred and the squeaking of tables and benches were as intolerable as nails on a chalkboard.

I realize now that what I was experiencing was pure panic. I could hear my heart battering my eardrums and tasted a sharp metallic tang which would stay with me for several days afterwards. I vaguely recollect strong arms pulling me back from the counsellor's bench, while I cursed and swore as much as my disconnected senses would allow. I could see the outlines of faces I recognized, kind Eva Adams reaching out in sympathy for my plight, her gestures comforting but fleeting. Gradually the brute force of my suppressors won out and I was dragged away.

I vaguely recollect a smile passing the lips of Julia Stott as she walked away from court that day. No compassion, no sense of guilt at having sealed my appalling fate, just satisfaction in the knowledge that she was now untouchable. I became 'Prisoner 4374' while she simply reinvented herself in a different town, under an assumed name.

If I had known then what I know now friend, I would have savored the meals of bread and meat handed out in Boone County Jail. At least they were warm and had an iota of seasoning. My bed was uncomfortable, being a simple iron cot, the blanket rough and moth-eaten, but that too was bearable compared to what I was to endure later that year, and of course for the many years yet to come.

I would have but twenty days to endure the confines of the jail and then I was to be taken to hell – Joliet State Penitentiary - for 'The term of my natural life'. As I was escorted away, I ruefully wondered how long that would be. I still had money in the bank, to which I had allowed my attorney access to pay for his services, and I had confidence that there would be enough for an appeal, a retrial, anything. But, as I turned to face Chas Fuller, I could see that he thought his work was done. Gather up the file and go home now Chas, your dishonorable client, Dr. Cream, is no longer in need of your ministrations!

Later, as I entered my cell that fateful night, on 31st October 1881, I started to recover my senses but still hardly registered what had happened. I found bruises upon my arms and my spine knotted in agony where some officer or another had felt obliged to stick their boot in me. I recalled that the journey from the courthouse back to Boone County Jail was but a short one, but every hole in the road seemed as though it had been positioned to exact as much discomfort as humanly possible.

It wasn't only the shock of my sentence friend, but something had been unleashed within me, something sinister and far darker than I had ever experienced before. As the warder turned the key, a different lock was opened, one deep inside me that opened a chasm of malevolence.

7

Joliet State Penitentiary, Illinois

On 1st November 1881, I entered a kind of Hades that I would never wish you to visit dear friend. If I had ever thought that I was treated with disdain in the Boone County Jail, well now I was something totally new, a number.

As Prisoner 4374, I was stripped of all my possessions and then stripped again, the second time literally, with a full body search followed by a freezing cold bucket of water thrown over me. I was presented with the kind of garb that only a coal miner or laborer might wear, given four candles as my monthly allowance of light source and shown to a grey cell in the main prison block. I was endowed with a list of rules to read and memorize, the like of which I had never been subjected to before. There I sat until it was time to march to the dinner hall, partially in disbelief that I was really to serve a life sentence here but also wondering how long it would be until help would come.

I had every faith that my brother Daniel would fight for my release, we might not have been close in recent years but the Cream family bond was still tight. There was also my attorney, who still had enough of my funds to petition for a retrial. I saw my hope as a flickering flame, at first it shone brightly with endurance and vigor, but gradually dimmed until the wind blew it out and there was little I could do to reignite the spark.

I am proud to report that I tolerated my circumstances reasonably well for the first few months. I was put to work in the general labor yard and fair enjoyed the regulations of strict silence. I had no desire to converse with the vagabonds around me and, given my rather laudable education, I cannot conceive what we might have possibly discussed even if we had been permitted to chat freely. I was surrounded by thieves, forgers and rapists who could write no more than ten letters between them if they tried, and physically I was of strong build in those days, not a man to bow to bullies, so all in all I was left to my own devices.

I was allowed access to the very limited source of books that the prison had to offer, which was at least some consolation. You may imagine, my dear friend, that my fellow criminals had no use for such literary delights, but I frequently found myself amongst scholars. Oh yes, there were schoolmasters, clerks and businessmen locked up amongst fraudsters, pillagers and murderers.

There was a clique of negro prisoners too, all protesting their innocence, but my they could work. I have never before witnessed such muscular torsos as those of my colored brethren.

With my medical knowledge, it was only a matter of time before the prison infirmary requested that I be put on their permanent shifts. Governor Ogilvy had other ideas however and refused me a position where I would be in daily contact with harmful chemicals. Given the nature of my 'supposed' crime, I guess I can hardly blame the man. Pity I couldn't put my talents to good use, it was most assuredly needed, what with all the brawls and attempted stabbings. I even heard of one fellow trying to puncture another chap's artery with a bent fork in the dinner hall. Despite my growing fears and boredom, I held my head up as best I could, and I would go about my daily grind with as little human interaction as possible.

My cell mate was an older man of indiscriminate nature, serving seven years for burglary. We sometimes talked in low tones in the evenings but even then it was ramblings about his family that carried the discourse rather than anything significant that I had to impart.

Each day merged in to the next, with only random visits from Chas Fuller to break up the monotony. One significant visit came early in 1882.

For months I had been corresponding by letter with my attorney, enticing him to comb Garden Prairie for further witnesses who may be able to testify against the reliability of Julia Stott's statements. And by God, one such gent did exist!

DeWitt J. Edgcomb was a neighbor and close friend of Daniel Stott at the stage of his untimely death. As I read through his sworn statement my heart lifted, here was the evidence we needed for my release and the prosecution of the Stott woman. Mr. Edgcomb declared that Mrs. Stott's conduct was such at the time of her husband's death that it led those close to her to believe that she had killed him. He further stated that he and others of the area knew Julia Stott well and would not believe her, even under oath. My mood was immediately lifted friend, all the authorities had to do was locate Julia Stott, arrest her and put her back on the stand.

If only life were that simple! Months went by and still no sign of that rancorous female could be found. Even days of hard labor in the freezing yard could not cleanse my nightmares. I dreamed of chasing a cloaked woman across the state night after night, never catching her but eternally hearing the laughter as she flitted away. I was even forced to part with good coin to send a private detective to join the search, but all to no avail. Julia Stott had covered her trail well, probably a scheme which she had rehearsed for months or maybe even years before we met.

There was no optimism left inside me. Without the star felon there could be no further trial. That meant no release, only years of penal servitude 'for the term of my natural life'.

In November 1884, life was to take a turn for the worse. I know how you smile at that phrase dear reader, was I not already keeping my head afloat in the depths of despair?

Well, let me tell you, given my muscular build and tall frame, I was a perfect candidate for transferal to the Granite Department where the toil was labor-intensive and even more repetitive than before. At nights, it was all I could do to lift a spoon to my mouth as my ligaments stretched and shifted from being wrenched for eight long hours. My previous experience of labor in the yard had been nowhere near as demanding as that which I now was forced to endure. Ironic to look back and think that, three years previously, I would have been writing prescriptions to soothe the ailments of my patients, whereas now I could do little to ease my own pain.

Day after day we were marched out to the vast expanse behind the prison where our tools and labor awaited. I noticed that some of the more mature prisoners were given menial tasks such as piling the smaller stones into mounds or repairing the broken picks and spades. Due to my relative youth, my tasks were usually comprised of smashing the large chunks of granite in to brick-sized pieces or wheeling full barrows from one side of the yard to another. It may sound an easy chore dear reader, but my spine tensed in spasms under the weight of each new load.

The dust too was hard to bear. It seemed to become ingrained in every orifice of my body and filled my lungs so that, if I happened to inhale too deeply, I would feel a choking sensation closing my airways.

Our clothing affected little protection against the conditions in which we toiled. Boots became ragged, trousers torn, and jackets stiff with the very earth of our labors. At the end of each new sunset, I would return along the same route, my hair and face white like some powdered ghoul, my hands blistered and bloody. This was no occupation for a gentleman of my standing in society and never a moment passed when I didn't regret my involvement with Julia Stott.

You may be mistaken in to thinking that my headaches were gone, as I have erred in keeping them muted, but no such luck had befallen me friend. As the syphilis spread deeply, like a leaking tap within my brain, the hallucinations began and the night terrors worsened. With no morphine to quell the pain, I began to have heavy migraines which left me so nauseous that I would be unable to eat for days. Convicts in the adjoining cells would complain harshly about my hollering, sometimes by banging their tin cups on the walls but mostly by pushing me deeply in the ribs during the march to our work area. My cell mate bemoaned to the warden about my midnight wailings and found himself moved to a cell with a more agreeable occupant. From then on, it appeared to me that the frequently changing tenants who were housed with me were there as punishment for insubordination or sometimes just pure ignorance.

Can you see how my countenance would deteriorate friend? Gradually I became a frail and wizened man compared to my former handsome self, poor hygiene of weekly bathing roughened the texture of my once smooth skin and, as a result of the infernal stress, I started to lose my hair. It sickened me to think that I had, in times gone by, been the center of attention for swarms of eligible young ladies on both sides of the Atlantic.

At the end of that year I received another visit by Chas Fuller, bringing overwhelming news that would set the course for my release. The aging attorney of Julia Stott, a Mr. O. H. Wright, had written a statement to the effect that he believed his client to be guilty, furthermore acquitting me of all involvement in the murder. Mr. Wright had even gone so far as to sign a petition in my favor, which was duly passed to the Governor to entreat him to scrutinize my case. Little did I realize the road to freedom would be far-reaching.

I guess at the time of these appeals I was a less than tenable man but you have to appreciate that my sense of time was exaggerated inside those stinking walls. Days felt like months and my sanity was like a fragile shard of glass just waiting to shatter. Hence, it is without bewilderment that I lashed out in frustration, refusing to subject myself to any kind of labor, and found myself in solitary confinement for seven days in April 1885. The punishment was not harsh for a man as stubborn as I, a dark cell with minimal rations, but some days they would handcuff me to the door with my arms raised and that alone instilled in me a reasoning to comply with the system. I confess to one further outburst in August of the same year but, after receiving another eight days in isolation, I returned to my chamber a more reserved and abiding individual.

During those torturous days I was ignorant of how many good fellows were submitting pleas for my liberation. There was even a submission from the office of the British Consul, on behalf of the Honorable Lionel Sackville-West no less! How fortunate to have friends in high places, but of course we chaps had made a pledge to a certain 'Society' and were bound by duty to help each other in an hour of need. I knew that somewhere 'R' would also be trying to assist my cause and gave silent thanks for true advocates of the brotherhood.

Have you ever been given a gift dear friend, only to open it up and find that it wasn't what you really wanted or that it was a cheaper version of the coveted item you drooled over in a shop window? Well now, times that feeling by ten and you will be close to my despondency and frustration at how unhurriedly the wheels of authority turned. You may be forgiven in your miscalculation of the judicial system workings, just as I underestimated my time still to be served.

It was to be another five and a half years until I finally heard word that the new administrator, Governor Fifer, had looked favorably upon the grounds for my release and a date for my deliverance was upon the horizon.

A sad twist of fate dampened my spirits at that time, as I was also to receive news that my father had passed away after a short but discomforting illness. I had been handsomely provided for in his will, a rather satisfactory sum of $16,000 was to be held in trust until such time as I could collect the currency myself. You see, despite the shame that had tarnished my family on my incarceration, my dear papa must have believed in my innocence, otherwise he would surely have cut me off without a cent would he not?

And so, at last the reprieve came, my freedom had been secured with assurances to the authorities (from my brother no less) that I would no longer burden the United States with my presence and upon release would seek passage to England.

As I trimmed my whiskers on that last morning in Joliet, 31st July 1891, I hardly recognized my reflection in the mirror. Gone was the successful doctor who could woo a maiden at ten yards, my complexion had yellowed and I now carried just half the bodyweight of previous years. As I slowly dressed in my suit of clothes that had been stored away in some dusty closet for the past decade, I pondered at how I would keep up my pants having lost my full waist and felt confounded at the way in which my jacket hung loosely around my once stoic shoulders. Yes, I was half the man who had been sent to trial but no amount of powdering or tailoring could ever erase the demon who struggled to free himself from the confines of my mind.

As I stepped through those heavy iron gates, I almost choked on the air. Fresh and sweet, no smell of stale sweat from toiling convicts, no greyness, only bright sunlight and floating clouds to penetrate my sight. Was this a dream?

Far from it friend, Dr. Cream was free and so too was the diabolic fiend that had been shackled for what had seemed like an eternity. Revenge on womankind was going to be so very sweet.

THOMAS NEILL CREAM 1874
MUSEE McCORD

ILLINOIS STATE PENITENTIARY.

DESCRIPTION OF CONVICT.

When Received _____ *November 1" 1884*

Registered No. _*4374*_ Name _*Thomas N Cream*_

Alias _____

County _*Boone*_ Term _*September*_

Crime _*Murder*_

Sentence _*His Natural Life*_

Age when received _*31*_ Nativity _*Scotland*_

Legitimate Occupation _*Physician*_

Height _*5* feet_ _*9* inches_ Complexion _*Medium dark*_

Color of Hair _*Brown*_ Color of Eyes _*Light gray*_

Social State _*Widower*_

Has Parents _*Father*_ Children _*None*_

Religion _*None*_ Habits of Life _*Moderate*_

Mental Culture _*Good*_ Tobacco _*Chew*_

Former Imprisonment _____

Name and address of nearest relation _*William Cream Fa*_ _*Quebec Can*_

GENERAL REMARKS.

Peculiarity in build and feature _*Stout solid build full face and forah*_ _*Hair quite thin on top and for part of head inch de*_ _Beard worn when received_ _*Auburn Mustache*_

Complexion slightly florid. Heavy whiskers, jaws and chin.

Size of Boot worn _*9*_ Weight _*182*_

India Ink marks _____

Scars and deformities _*Deep scar on left side of abdomen says*_ _*Caused by a surgical operation*_

CONVICT DESCRIPTION 1884
ILLINOIS STATE ARCHIVES

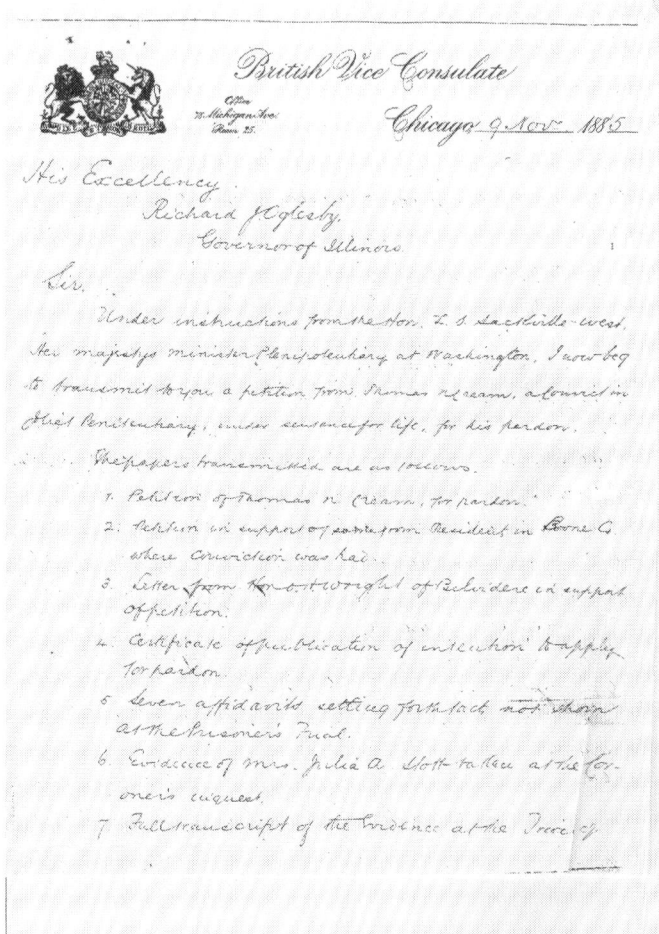

British Vice Consulate

Office
75 Michigan Ave.
Room 25.

Chicago 9 Nov. 1885

His Excellency.
   Richard J. Oglesby.
      Governor of Illinois.

Sir.

   Under instructions from the Hon. L. S. Sackville-West. Her Majesty's minister Plenipotentiary at Washington. I now beg to transmit to you a petition from Thomas N. Cream, a convict in Joliet Penitentiary, under sentence for life, for his pardon.

   The papers transmitted are as follows.

   1. Petition of Thomas N. Cream, for pardon.
   2. Petition in support of same from Resident in Boone Co. where conviction was had.
   3. Letter from Hon. orit wright of Belvidere in support of petition.
   4. Certificate of publication of intention to apply for pardon.
   5. Seven affidavits setting forth facts not shown at the Prisoner's Trial.
   6. Evidence of Mrs. Julia A. Stott taken at the foroner's inquest.
   7. Full transcript of the Evidence at the Trial of

LETTER FROM THE BRITISH VICE CONSUL 1885
ILLINOIS STATE ARCHIVES

LETTER FROM DANIEL CREAM 1889
ILLINOIS STATE ARCHIVES

Illinois State Penitentiary,

WARDEN'S OFFICE,

Joliet, Ill. *May 22* 1891

Hon *Chas E Fuller,*

Springfield Ill.

Sir:—

In response to *your request* I have the honor to furnish Certificate of the conduct of convict *Thos N Cram* Reg. No. *4374* who, as appears of record, was received in this institution *November 1* 18*81* from the *September* term of the *Circuit* Court of *Boone* County, under sentence of *Life* years, for the crime of *Murder*

It appears of record that, to this date, *he has lost* _____ *of his good time* _____

That he was punished for the following offenses:—
April 28' 1885 – Spoiling work – 7 days in Solitary
August 13' 1885 – Not doing reasonable work - 8 days in _____

For minor offenses against the Rules and Regulations for the Government of Convicts he has been

Reported and excused: *four times*

Reported and temporarily deprived of privilege to write, to receive visits from friends, etc., _____

Reported and disciplined by short detention in solitary: *twice*

Since *the 20' of June 1888* his conduct has *been good*

Very respectfully,

Your obedient servant,

Henry D Dement

WARDEN.

CERTIFICATE OF CONDUCT 1891
ILLINOIS STATE ARCHIVES

8

Daniel's House, Quebec

Focus your mind, dear friend, on the journey that lay ahead of me. Never before had I experienced such personal degradation and lack of compassion. I was well aware of my ill-fitting clothes and fraying cuffs, but my fellow passengers made sure that I knew my position aboard that carriage. Even the farm laborers visiting kin in far off states cast their eyes downwards on meeting my eye.

My fare allowed me standard travel and an overnight bunk as we headed north to Canada. Not that I should sleep as we crossed the border to my homeland. I spent hour after hour watching the passing countryside turn from burnt yellow to bright green, passengers came and went, conversations drifted to silence.

My gut lurched and twisted at what I should find at the end of the line. It had been a long time since any of my family had sent messages of good will. I knew that Daniel had done all that a brother could in terms of fighting for my freedom, but not once had he stepped foot inside Joliet. He had not yet witnessed the premature ageing that had changed me beyond recognition, nor had he been there to bring new medication to control my everlasting migraines. Still, his ceaseless petitioning had served me well.

As I stood upon the threshold of my brother's home, I was unaware of the impact that my appearance would have on the family inside. I must have cut quite a shabby character, what with my over-sized suit, sallow skin and lack of hair. My only luggage was a small brown paper parcel which carried the few meagre items I had on my person at the time of my arrest all those years ago. So here I stood, Uncle Thomas the criminal had come to stay. Of course, Daniel had sent a letter bidding me to visit, but in all honesty where else was I to go? I had a younger sister, Rachel, of whom I was very fond, but I really could do without the sympathy and pampering to which I knew she would be prone.

Nothing could prepare me for the unsettling look on Daniel's face as he greeted me, it was part disbelief but with a faint glimmer of recognition. He must have anticipated that the years inside Joliet's unforgiving walls would change me, but he had obviously underestimated the degree of deterioration. Nevertheless, forever the perfect host, my brother took me in a hearty embrace and ushered me inside. There must have been some semblance of shame, as I was led upstairs to my room where I was hurriedly poured a hot bath and issued with a new set of clothes. I confess, it felt good to be really clean again, but no amount of scrubbing would cleanse the thirst for vengeance bubbling just below the surface of my skin.

That evening I went down to dinner where Jessie, my sister-in-law, and the children were seated. The two youngest I had never met (with me being a trifle preoccupied at the time of their births) but it didn't stop their questions and sidelong glances. Daniel had employed a good cook but her talents were wasted on me I'm afraid, as my appetite was meagre and my stomach weak. As I pushed the food around my plate, Daniel tried his best to make light conversation but, being all too aware of the disdainful looks around the table, I excused myself and retired to bed.

I do not blame my brother for his choice of bride, after all she had fulfilled her role as heir provider quite adequately, but I cared little for that woman. No fancy dresses or golden ringlets could disguise her true intention: to spend her husband's hard earned dollars as if money were rapidly going out of fashion. I had no care for her thoughts on my arrival either, I would make Daniel's home my temporary sanctuary until such time as I could collect my inheritance and arrange passage to England where my true friends were.

Those first few weeks were all to be concentrated on my careful preparation. Firstly I had Daniel secure me a prescription to ease my migraines. At least if I could keep them under control during the daytime I would have clarity in thinking, something which had evaded me for some time. I also ordered a tonic to help build up my strength, after all dear reader, the brute force needed to carry out my impending scheme was essential. Ha, ha, wondering what I have in store for you? Be patient friend, all will be revealed in good time.

As I ventured in to town on Daniel's insistence, I reflected upon my days in Chicago and how flippant I had been in ordering the best of everything, from wine to boots. This time, I had an obligation to only line my trunk with the necessary closet of a gentleman at leisure. Therefore, I spent several days in selecting the finest silk for my two top hats and a few afternoons in discussion with the tailor who was to supply me with three excellent suits, the very things which would add credibility to my new identity as a professional abroad.

Initially I had to borrow funds from my brother, but only under the premise that on settlement of father's will, he would be reimbursed fully. However, despite the knowledge that I would soon be in a position to repay my debt tenfold, every day that I had to beg cash from Daniel felt like one more year that we grew farther apart. Some evenings, I admit, I would loiter at the bottom of the stair after dinner to hear Daniel and Jessie bicker about my plight. Needless to say, 'family' always prevailed and despite his wife's misgivings, Daniel was always ready to write out a money order in my favor.

My brother had also been so good as to collect my belongings from my chambers in Chicago when all that trouble first arose, so now I carefully picked out the items which I would need on my journey, and discarded those which either no longer fitted me or would serve no purpose in my new life overseas.

The most important article, still blissfully intact, was my leather-bound medical case. I remember a cursory smile playing on my lips as I carefully opened the lid and peeked inside. There were all the little glass vials, lined up neatly like a legion of centurions standing to attention. I ran a calloused finger along the labels and read them aloud in delight : STRYCHNINE, CANNABIS, QUININE, DOVER POWDER, and look right there my very favorite, NUX VOMICA. Why was it my most coveted drug? Because of its effects, dear reader. I forget, you are probably not a medic such as I, you see Nux Vomica was strychnine in the purest form. Just a few drops were guaranteed to bring severe cramps, lock-jaw and then death all within twenty minutes. Quite an effective poison don't you think? Don't roll your eyes, you knew I had a devilish plan, so that makes you an accomplice! But let us not get ahead of ourselves, there was plenty more to do before the hunt could commence. Firstly, I had to convince brother dearest to have my precious vials refilled with fresh ingredients as I couldn't risk a decade of storage lessening the effect of the 'medicine' now could I?

I spent a couple of very frustrating months holed up in that house. When Daniel had business to attend to I would purposely feign a migraine and either lock myself in my room or take a long walk in the suburbs. Anything, just to get out of the sight of that darned bitch. I can't say it was any one aspect of Jessie's pathetic existence that riled me, just the fact that she was a woman sufficed. Every hand she laid upon my brother's shoulder, every gesture as she smoothed her gown, all of these things reminded me vividly of my days in courtship with Julia Stott.

Ten years is a long time to harbor hate. Ten years that can neither be returned nor relived, an eternity of schemes to be pursued and nightmares to be put to rest. Suddenly it all became clear, women had been my undoing since the very first time I slipped my juvenile hand beneath some whore's petticoats. Nothing constructive had ever come from any of my liaisons had they? Flora, Lena, Julia….she-devils!

As for the dirty harlot who had infected me with her disease, the reason for my deteriorating mind, I hoped she had befallen some vile and excruciating fate. In that split second I knew that the only pleasure I could glean from life would be to rid the world of as many of those disgusting women as possible, starting with the street-walkers. What better place to find a plentiful supply of prostitutes in 1891 than good old London? And so my plan was forged.

With Daniel's guidance, I secured the funds left to me by my father and took some comfort in the knowledge that I could cross the ocean a wealthy man. I would have no need to find employment unless I so desired and determined to secure myself mediocre lodgings in the heart of the East End as soon as I arrived.

I was eager to reacquaint myself with chums from my early days in London but nervous too that they may be alarmed at my countenance. I reasoned that news of my imprisonment would surely have been hot gossip in England, especially among the medical crowd, and concluded to keep a low profile until such time as I was convinced my associates were genuine allies. Despite my innocence, circulars always reported on the macabre and I had no desire to have my soon-to-be victims alerted to my identity. Therefore, I would adopt my middle name as the last and become Dr. T. Neill.

I was under no illusion that stepping back on to the streets of London would be just like the good old days. Those capers were just a distant memory now but I felt some degree of excitement as I tried to recall the music halls and public houses of days gone by.

I wondered how my chum 'R' had fared in my absence. He had been enduring domestic problems of his own at our last meeting and I genuinely hoped that life had dealt him a good hand while I'd been away. We were two of a kind 'R' and I, both ambitious and personable in our own different ways, but firm friends who understood the implications of lending a hand to a fellow in need.

Of course, I had no idea of his whereabouts now. It was unlikely that he would still be at the same address but, if he was moving in medical circles, a few discreet questions in the right ears might point me in his direction. I could imagine that 'R' probably had a few tales of his own to tell and some light-hearted distraction would be a welcome tonic while I settled in to my new surroundings. I debated whether I should share my plans with him or wait until I had subdued my first victim.

A brotherhood like ours had a strong bond and I was satisfied that we shared a common enough animosity towards women that he would applaud my motives and maybe even offer to lend a hand.

Early September 1891, I said my last farewell to Daniel and thanked him heartily for his support. I was at last feeling stronger, physically anyhow, my mental state could only be determined by those who interacted with me at the time. I certainly felt able to provide for myself now and a fresh start was something I looked forward to with relish.

As I boarded the S.S. Teutonic, my fellow passengers were unaware of the large quantities of drugs stowed safely in my luggage. Enough to poison every one of them should I so desire but it was important to keep a low profile on the journey. I may have had one weak moment during those days at sea however, as upon arrival in Liverpool Docks, should you happen to count those precious vials once again, you would notice one lonely tube sitting empty among his fully replenished brothers. Don't frown dear reader, it was simply for practice, and not a very significant traveler if I remember rightly. Just some bitch who looked at me with contempt. Oh don't worry, I was quite careful in the administration to the dear woman's drink, her vomiting and early demise were attributed to bad oysters from the buffet. I lost no sleep, it was necessary rehearsal for my cleansing of the London streets. Made sense for me to have a little 'trial' don't you think? No pun intended ha, ha!

Dr. T. Neill really had quite a sadistic persona didn't he?

The trip from Liverpool to London was uneventful apart from a heavy rainstorm, reminding me how I might have missed these golden shores but certainly not the dire British weather. Still, there was work to be done and nothing could deter me from my mission.

I checked in to Anderton's Hotel in Fleet Street at first, as I needed a few days to seek out desirable lodgings and order some suitable attire. After all, if I was to live the life of a prestigious doctor I should dress the part accordingly.

My days in Quebec with Daniel had served me well, and I now looked groomed and much healthier than when I had left the fortified walls of Joliet some months before. With the aid of regular opiates, I could control my night terrors to some degree and the incessant shaking, that had plagued me for years, became nothing more than a slight tremor.

With my newly found purpose and ambition I set forth in to the slums of Lambeth to seek accommodation. You may wonder why I chose not to search wealthier, less seedier areas of the city, but this was the place best-known to me. These streets held some of my best memories, along with my favorite haunts. The perfect place for a perfect murder, or two!

9

Anderton's Hotel, fleet Street, London

These were exciting times, Friend. I had the bowels of London at my fingertips and a new found purpose positively glowing inside me. My rooms at Anderton's were most pleasing, being both comfortable and in a central location from which I could dally forth in to the labyrinth of shoddy terraced houses and ale-sodden inns. I filled my lungs with the scents around me: hop yards, jam and pickle factories and fish shops, quite a unique combination but, ultimately, the smell of poverty. London was a heaven for those wishing to experience hell, and that was just what I had in mind! I still had plans to locate 'R' but, not knowing where to start, that was a task which would have to wait until I was properly settled. Besides it would be much more fun to raise our glasses to a toast after my successful eradication of a few Lambeth street-walkers, a plan that 'R' himself had out-lined to me over a decade before. Whether it had been in pure jest I am not at liberty to tell.

And so, after more than a decade of dreams and serious calculation, I had returned to the city of gold. Can you put yourself in my position, dear friend? Luxury accommodation, plush velvet curtains to close out the turmoil from the street below and most of all anonymity. You see that was the all-important factor, that nobody knew me, recognized me or had ever read about Dr. Neill. I was free to pursue my passions.

Anderton's knew how to make a chap feel like royalty. My room was furnished to the highest degree, my bathroom complete with fragrant French soaps. My, did I feel like a king. Any woman should have been overjoyed to stay in such a sublime sanctuary, should I have chosen a lady to share my delightful surroundings. But I am a predator, or so you should have gathered by now. I would never open my bedchamber to any old slut, unless of course the whore in question was about to meet her end with me, ha, ha!

Do not perceive me as a criminal, I sought only to carry out my innocuous deeds upon the fallen wenches who spread their filthy afflictions to honorable gents like myself. It was only natural that I should lie in wait until the very best opportunity presented itself.

On the dreary fall evening of Tuesday 6th October 1891, the day after my arrival in London, I stepped out in to the relentless rain in search of my first victim. Well, I say victim, but what I really needed to do was stake out a few locations and see just where those drunken harlots plied their wares. It had also been over a decade since I had satisfied the stirrings in my loins and despite the disease coursing inside me, some quick release would be a comfort. Earlier that day I had ingested a few grains of morphine, just as a tonic mind, to help brighten my mood and to keep my head from pounding as the hours passed. And so, being extremely careful to avoid the splashes from passing carriages, and with no particular destination in mind, I found myself strolling across to Ludgate Circus. Despite the rainstorm pounding the cobblestones there were plenty of young women advertising their trade. No, I shouldn't call them women as such, strumpets may be a better word to describe those fallen creatures. Some were lonely old sots, with pock-marked complexions and grease-stained blouses, just begging for the opportunity to earn a few shillings to pay for their next drink. I had nothing against those old dears, well nothing a handful of lethal strychnine granules wouldn't sort out, but a fellow has to have standards. It may puzzle you to think of me with a certain type of prostitute on my target list, but it simply wouldn't be fun to eradicate the old bitches who were just one bottle of gin away from their grave anyway. Besides, it may become necessary to get physically intimate with one, or more, of them . A chap had to keep certain ethics, even if his morals were a little frayed around the edges.

Now don't imagine that I had attempted to regain my handsome looks and professional gait of days gone by. I was all too aware that I had changed. But when a fellow is going to pay for services from a street-walker, she looks past the thinning hair and pallid skin. No mind is given to the deep circles around a chap's eyes and certainly no comment is made in regard to a customer's attire. Instead it is the depth of a gentleman's purse and the speed with which he can satisfy his sexual cravings that attracts those dirty whores. In this I was a master of disguise, allowing those poor degenerates to see me as a man of wealth trapped in a marriage of convenience, seeking comfort in the bosom of a sympathetic maiden.

As I turned up the collar on my woollen cape, a rather pretty young wench caught my eye. She was dressed much less shabbily than the others that night, with a wide-brimmed hat that matched her long green skirt, exactly the same color as her feline-shaped eyes. Turns out, her name was Elizabeth Masters but being a close acquaintance by the end of that night, I got to call her Liz.

The rain showed no signs of letting up that evening, so I suggested we take shelter in the nearby 'King Lud' public-house. We had to raise our voices considerably in order to converse with each other over the noise but Liz was only too happy to enjoy the warmth of that establishment while I plied her with wine and tales of my exploits as a doctor at St. Thomas's. She really was a polite young thing and listened intently as I made up a tale that I had come to London to claim some inherited property, she even cooed over photographs of my mother, which in hindsight I really should not have been flashing about. After finishing two bottles of cheap red wine, I proposed that we get down to business. After all, what purpose is there in wasting good coin on a prostitute unless a fellow intends to get his money's worth eh? With that, Liz walked me to her room at No.9 Orient Buildings in Hercules Road, an area I knew of old, with it being just off Lambeth Road. The place was basic but incredibly clean and I couldn't help but wonder what circumstances had befallen this girl to see her making her living in this way. Oh, don't worry dear reader, I am not about to turn soft and sympathetic, it was just a momentary thought which soon passed to the back reaches of my memory.

I won't bore you with the details of my lusty escapades that night, but let's just say that the whore new which areas of my anatomy needed her attention and I was soon feeling a great deal more satisfied than when I had arrived. As a token of my appreciation, as well as the usual fee for services partaken of course, I offered to accompany Liz to Gatti's Music Hall for a couple of hours, where we could make merry and soak up the atmosphere around us. Oh, how good to be back in London again! I felt positively delirious. On arriving at Gatti's we were joined by Elizabeth May, a good friend of Liz Masters who, despite being less attractive than her co-worker, was fairly pleasing to the eye. Just a pity we hadn't bumped in to her earlier I say, could have got twice the service for just a little more cash! Ha, gently does it Dr. Neill, no need to get greedy dear chap!

At around 2am, I bid farewell to those raucous bitches, promising to write to Liz with arrangements for another meeting when I had secured myself in lodgings, and made haste towards my hotel. You see, friend, she had come to no harm! But next time the little whore might not be so lucky. I had gone out to scout around, leaving behind my medicine bag and not really intending to murder that night. My game plan was still very much on track and that night's research had been invaluable. I now knew how easy it would be to entice the next hooker, the location of a suitable alleyway should I rapidly need to dispose of a body and most importantly how to get satisfaction without any emotional involvement.

Another shift came over my countenance that night dear friend. Perhaps it was the disease rearing its ugly head or maybe it was my conscience bugging me but, on returning to my suite, I battled with the urge to scrub every inch of my skin until no trace of my dirty encounter survived. I could feel the battle inside me, and the next few months were going to be long and arduous if I didn't get a firm grip on my inner demon.

I slept fitfully again that night, tossing and turning until it was no use and I was forced to rise from the comfort of my bed and accept that slumber had defeated me. My escapades of the previous evening had fuelled my appetite and I ate a hearty English breakfast in the dining room. I don't know whether the depravity of mealtimes in Joliet had altered my taste buds, or the English simply know how to laden their tables, but that morning I dined on the best pork sausages I'd ever tasted and washed them down with fragrant Earl Grey tea. It set me up perfectly for my next task, which was to call upon a lodging house at 103 Lambeth Palace Road, with a view to finding my new abode. I am sure that, should my fellow hotel guests have suspected where I was to lay my hat for the next twelve months they would have either entreated me to reconsider or looked upon me as some half-wit in need of urgent indoctrination.

The stroll across Westminster Bridge was a breezy one but I much preferred to travel on foot rather than hansom-cab as it would ingrain a mental map in my head should I ever need to retrace my steps in haste. These were the streets that would become my hunting ground, the tall buildings would cast long shadows across my deeds and hopefully I would be safely on my way before folks became alerted to any infringement of the law. This was the ideal setting for my vengeful scheme and I sincerely hoped that I would not encounter any infractions to cause me delay.

I had carefully thought through my guise and, when Miss. Sleaper the landlady's rather dim-witted daughter showed me to the available quarters, I recounted how I was an American surgeon seeking rest and recuperation in England's most glorious city. The foolish girl didn't question my motives in wanting to convalesce in one of the smoggiest, foul-aired streets of London. She simply smiled and reached out her hand to collect the bundle of notes with which I offered to pay three months' rent in advance and dutifully called for a cab to collect my belongings from Anderton's. Life was so easy when you just knew how to handle people. As it turned out I wasn't the only medic to be leasing rooms from the Sleaper family, but all will be explained on that note a little later dear friend.

Now, a doctor who intends to practice on his personal premises needs rooms that differ to those in private employment. Therefore, my lodgings were mediocre but sufficed perfectly for the purpose which they were intended – a dry roof over my head, laundering of my clothes and a hot meal every once in a while.

For the latter, I only intended to dine at home on Sunday evenings, it being the finale to a busy week and the evening of which I was most likely to be taking a rest from my physical exertions in the city.

I cannot, in all honesty, complain. Mrs. Sleaper was a good soul and kept her house immaculate, albeit sparse. I immediately purchased several academic volumes with which to line the bookshelves in my room and my good landlady agreed to spruce up the décor by giving both the eiderdown and window dressings a good beating in the yard outside. I don't remember ever having the fortune of meeting Mr. Sleaper, a hard-working and mild-mannered man by all accounts, but I was often to hear the tread of his step as he returned home after a long day at his labor.

For now I will leave you with the vision of Dr. Thomas Neill relaxing in front of a roaring fire, with legs stretched out akimbo, boots strewn across the floor and a good book at his side. A plentiful supply of opiates lined the infamous medical bag and a fully replenished stream of murderous deeds furnished the good doctor's dreams. Life was grand, and it was just about to get better.

10

103, Lambeth Palace Road, London

I had been enjoying the comfort of my new home for just a couple of days when I started to think about my jolly night with Liz. She had been rather good company and I thought it might be fun to repeat our antics, although at that point I was undecided as to whether the girl would live afterwards or not. Therefore I put pen to paper and sent her a short note, suggesting that I call on her between three and five that very afternoon.

My plan for the morning was to attend to an issue that had been bothering me for some time. My eyesight had been deteriorating slowly for a while, partly due to short-sightedness from birth, but I was also convinced that the wretched syphilis was starting to take its toll on my pupils as well. Whilst staying at Anderton's Hotel, I had noticed James Aitchison's optician shop just a few doors away, in Fleet Street, and the fellow seemed to be very popular with the affluent gents of society. Luckily I was able to be seen straight away and, after a thorough examination, it was decided that I needed two new pairs of spectacles. With any luck the prescription lenses would help to correct my worsening squint and improve my vision quite significantly. I duly paid the clerk and was informed that I would receive a package in about a week. All was fine and dandy, another problem solved.

On returning along the route to my lodgings, I decided to partake of a little lunch and a draught of ale. There were plenty of public houses to choose from, and presently I was tucking in to a meat and potato pie with a mug of beer to help it down. Maybe I was in high spirits that day, or perhaps fate came to lend a hand but the opportunity to claim my first English victim presented itself within minutes of me finishing my meal. Her name was Matilda Clover. From the outset I could see that the woman was an alcoholic, the fact that she was drinking in an alehouse early afternoon was a big clue, but she was young enough and not too displeasing to look at either. I didn't even need to charm my way into her trust, the promise of lining her pockets with a few shillings and a bottle of Guinness was enough for her to lead me back to her room. Now it just so happened that Matilda resided at No. 27 Lambeth Road, a house of multiple occupancy that faced directly on to Hercules Road, where I had previously spent a few hours in carnal mischief with Liz. However, despite my promises made earlier in the day, at that precise moment I had forgotten my appointment with Miss. Masters and focused all of my attention on the task at hand. Now you may be expecting to hear that Matilda Clover met her maker that dreary October afternoon but once again I had to let my victim go free. Blame it on too much ale or not enough morphine but, my friend the fact is, I just wasn't ready to go through with the homicide. Somehow I just needed to be in a more euphoric state of mind but never fear the right time would come soon, I could feel it in my bones. So, a couple of hours after our first acquaintance, I left Matilda in a state of undress and headed back to my rooms to mull over the day's events.

For the next few days my thoughts were in turmoil. I hardly slept as my night terrors took a gruesome turn for the worse and I knew that my condition was nearing its peak. I don't know if you have close family members who have contracted syphilis dear friend, probably not. You see it is a dreadfully debilitating disease, the ultimate state being called 'General Paralysis of the Insane', wherefore the mind becomes demented and the body is afflicted with seizures and all manner of sporadic jerks. I estimated that the canker had been within me for the best part of thirteen years, but I had enough medical knowledge to assess that it was starting to eat away at my senses and soon I would lose control of my ability to think rationally. Do not pity me, for I still had enough passion in me to carry out my murderous deeds as planned. Nothing would deter me from my mission. I just needed to channel the little energy that I had left and teach those dirty whores a lesson. However, I knew that eventually I would die, bedridden disorientated and alone.

By 13ᵗʰ October I was feeling slightly better, having had a few days rest and a strong concoction of my usual remedy. I arose quite early and despite the cold wind and grey skies, hailed a hansom cab, alighting at Priest's Pharmacy in Parliament Street. I was unknown to the assistant, John Kirkby, but soon gained his trust by explaining that I was attending a course of lectures at St. Thomas's Hospital and needed to purchase a quantity of Nux Vomica to enhance my experiments. He seemed unperturbed by my request but, as the gelatin capsules that I also required were out of stock, duly sent off an order to procure the items for me. I then set off for the York Hotel, in Waterloo Road where I booked a room in anticipation of my forthcoming crime.

Once again, fate crossed my path that very afternoon and I was soon conversing with a dainty wench named Ellen Donworth. We arranged to meet at the hotel at 6pm that very evening, I mean why delay? This time I would be prepared. Sure enough, Ellen arrived at the appointed hour and made herself comfortable on the beautifully embroidered chaise longue. I myself had arrived an hour earlier, intent upon mixing a suitable draught of brocine and strychnine to administer when the time felt right. Being a charmer, and not a complete cad by the way, we chatted for some time about her life on the streets and the circumstances which had forced her to be there. You see friend, it's all about gaining a victim's trust.

After a quick tussle on the bed, I reached out and offered the girl a drink from my bottle of creamy white tonic, "specially prepared to clear the complexion and brighten the skin". She didn't hesitate, ha, ha, and took a large gulp, only pausing momentarily to bemoan the sour taste.

Now the last thing I wanted to do was cause a scandal in the hotel, let alone have myself arrested for murder too soon so, knowing that I probably had around thirty minutes before the bitch would start convulsing, I suggested we go for a quick drink at the Wellington Public House. One glass of stout later, I left our little street-walker propped up against a lamp-post outside and walked briskly away. The last thing I remember hearing was her first cry of agony as the stomach cramps started and the poison worked its magic.

And so, I had done it! So easily duped and so easily dead! The next one would be even better. I took heed of the comment made by Ellen that the tonic had a sour taste and determined to wait until the gelatin capsules had arrived before I sought out my next victim. It would take little coaxing to get them to swallow a pill that looked like it had been professionally prepared, besides with my first conquest out of the way I should rejoice, take a little 'Me' time. And I knew exactly what I needed to do next.

For the next few days I carefully scrutinized the London newspapers for reports on Ellen Donworth's early demise. There were but a few paragraphs detailing her last agonizing moments and then finally, on the third day, a Coroner's verdict of 'Death by strychnine and morphia administered by persons unknown'. Shortly afterwards a jeweler's traveling salesman was arrested but soon released without charge.

You may call me egotistic dear reader, but maybe there was simply an underlying urge to be captured, as my next move was one far more daring than simply poisoning a hooker. I decided to pen a letter to George Wyatt, the Deputy Coroner who had officiated at Ellen Donworth's inquest.

Posing as a private detective, I carefully disguised my shaky handwriting as I formed the words: "I am willing to say that if you and your satellites fail to bring the murderer of Ellen Donworth, alias Linnell, to justice, I am willing to give you such assistance…provided your Government is willing to pay me $300,000 for my services. No pay if not successful."

I signed it 'A. O'Brien' and then waited, perusing the papers for a response, but none came.

Following my first successful poisoning, I was most definitely on a high. I tried to reason with myself, I should wait, take a short break and plan carefully. But thoughts of Matilda Clover filled my dreams. I knew where to find her and I knew she trusted me.

On 20th October 1891, I casually dropped by the alehouse where I had first spied Matilda sipping her gin and ruefully eying the gents in search of a likely punter. She recognized me at once and suggested we go back to her place for more drinks and whatever else I required. This time the house was occupied by more than a few residents and we were noticed by several passing occupants. One girl in particular stood peering at us as we passed, but Matilda told me to pay no attention to Lucy Rose, a mere servant employed to do laundry and clean house. Nevertheless, I pulled down the brim of my elegant silk hat so as not to be seen too clearly and passed by in to Matilda's open doorway.

This time, having carefully prepared the capsules that very afternoon, I passed off the pills as a gift. It would work wonders on the girl's pimpled cheeks and give her a glow that others would envy! Ha, ha, she nearly snatched my hand off in her haste to ingest my offerings! By the time we parted company it was past midnight and the house was quieter, so I carefully crept down the staircase and let myself out into the street. It wouldn't be long until the entire household would be awoken to the screams of a dying whore.

Again I scanned the periodicals for news of the street-walkers death, a task which the attending physician had obviously failed to do, otherwise he may have noted the similarities between Matilda Clover and Ellen Donworth's symptoms. One week after her supposed death from 'a lethal mixture of sedatives and brandy', Matilda Clover was buried in a pauper's grave at Tooting Cemetery.

You may be wondering how I knew where the poor girl was buried? Well, besides the obvious reports in the daily newspapers, I made enquiries at the morgue. It was rather a game actually, as the Coroner's assistant asked whether I was perhaps her family physician.

I do not know what division of my madness persuaded me to take a carriage out to Tooting. Perhaps I needed to satisfy myself that number two was really deceased. I was relatively new to the art of poisoning in London, despite my professional relationship with toxins, and had to be sure that my work was complete. And so, the finale to my deed was to witness the little wooden marker that denoted the resting place of Matilda Clover.

I can read your thoughts, friend. What about my many years behind bars for the very same crime? Well, please believe me, I was innocent of that atrocity as I have told you amongst these pages more times than I care to recall.

And so, there I stood, on the rain-soaked ground, looking down at my handiwork. My only fixed emotion that day was pride, pride in the knowledge that I had cleansed one more street corner and put those other dirty bitches on high alert. Oh they should watch out, for soon I would strike again.

Imagine my frustration at the authorities, friend. Nobody was searching for the killer! I had to take matters in to my own hands again, at least to keep those nitwits on their toes.

This time I targeted the newsagent family of W.H.Smith & Son, with an aim to incriminate their son in Ellen's death.

Why the Smith family? You are fully entitled to ask dear reader, although I could scour my logic for decades and still be unable to give you a watertight response. I suppose they were known to me by all the advertising I had seen in the London press, and what better way for my misdemeanors to gain publicity than through the channels of a newsagent?

It was an absolute plethora of delight to embark on such playful penmanship. I could well imagine the shock and horror on the faces of those accused and detailed carefully how Ellen Donworth had been in possession of two letters incriminating Smith beyond doubt. Apparently the death had caused a great sensation in the local community and my letter further fuelled the fire, dubbing the case 'The Lambeth Mystery'. My efforts proved to be less than fruitful however, as by the time Messrs. Smith had finally posted a small column in reply to my demands, I had lost my focus and moved my attention to more exciting pursuits. Oh, how easily my mind wandered in those first few months. I was hardly finishing one deed before another more illustrious proposition presented itself. Of course the increasing doses of toxic substances have played an undisclosed part in the ramblings of my brain.

Days would pass where I felt as happy as a lark, euphoric at times, but then ultimately the 'high' would take a dive and from then I would become somber and weak until the next hit. In modern times I may be labelled as a drug-addict but, you know dear friend, it wasn't too bad a title to possess in those times. Every man in the East End of London had his own personal vices, for some it was the opium pipe or a pinch of laudanum, whilst for others it was a bottle of boot-legger's gin.

Perhaps it was this instability that tamed my bravado and brought me to my senses again but, whatever the cause, I listened to the voice of reason and decided on a sojourn to the countryside to recharge my spirits.

11

Berkhampsted, Hertfordshire

As I feel we have now become close dear reader, I will allow you to see the other side of my complex personality. Would you like to see my romantic side? It is probably hard for you to imagine me wooing and courting a woman through genuine passion and intent. No turn of events can change a man's heart when he finds the right match, and find it I did in the arms of the beautiful Laura Sabbatini.

I had meant to visit Berkhamsted simply to take the air and gather my thoughts in light of recent circumstances but, being a man who enjoys society and gaiety, I decided to attend a local theatre show where it just so happened that the love of my life was waiting. As luck would have it our seats were next to each other and many meaningful glances were exchanged that night. Of course the dear young lady was not alone on her outing and was accompanied by her aging mother, a woman who thankfully was as deaf as a post and could not hear our idle chatter as we slowly became acquainted. I became entranced by Laura's tumbling black curls and arched brows, even the way she pulled on her silk gloves had a sensuous quality. I was totally smitten.

I will not bore you with the intimate details of our subtle courtship, besides these are moments that I wish to keep securely locked in my heart, but I will tell you that I fell for that girl as surely as if I'd been hit by a thunderbolt. I sincerely believe that Laura loved me in return and, if life had dealt me a different hand, I would have married her within the year.

Now you may be thinking dark thoughts about me friend, was there an ulterior motive for my pursuance of this wonderful creature? I suppose you think that there may have been an inheritance to have or a sizeable family estate to make my own, perhaps generations of diamonds and pearls or a fortune in bonds squirreled away in the bank? You would be wrong, so wrong, on all counts! Miss Sabbatini came from a working-class family with sound Christian ethics, nothing at all for my purse to get excited about. So, why now and why her?

I don't expect you to understand, but all I wanted was a good wife. Someone to love and cherish, and to be there in my final hours, when the disease finally took me. Of course I had no intention of telling Laura about my secret illness, I couldn't possibly risk losing her because of a mistake made over a decade before. She would never marry a man who was destined for insanity.

Laura had such passion when she talked about her dreams. She wanted to become a designer of dresses in London's fashionable West End and how I hoped I could fulfill those wishes. Nothing would be too good for my darling. Somehow we would be happy, if only for a while.

Within days of meeting my love, it became apparent to me that the palpitations in my heart could only be calmed when Laura was near, and so I took the rather bold step of moving myself out of the comfortable little hotel in the center of town and in to a small guest house just doors away from where my beloved was residing in Chapel Street.

It wasn't long before Mrs. Sabbatini was regularly inviting me to dine with her, and my darling of course. This was a whole new chapter in my life. Without appearing an infinite snob, I must explain that throughout my childhood we had house servants who cooked and cleaned under my mother's instruction. What I was to experience in the Sabbatini residence was something entirely different. Of course, they had a young girl who helped with domestic chores but, when we sat down to dinner, it was Laura's fair hand that served out the meat and vegetables.

One could not help but notice the little chips and cracks that defaced the family's fine porcelain and despite the silverware gleaming with the efforts of fervent polishing, there was a significant air of lost wealth in that home. Not that I cared to be in the company of less affluent ladies, not with my darling girl fluttering her eyelashes across the table. I was at the very pinnacle of my happiest times.

I spent many evenings in the Sabbatini household and, over the next three months, even accompanied the ladies to church service on Sundays. It was just as important for me to show how upright and respectable I was to Laura's mother, as you will appreciate. With her husband passed on, Mrs. S was the head of the roost and watched her daughter's every move like a beady-eyed crow. As it turned out I had no reason to worry, as my intended's mother thought it wonderful that her only daughter might become betrothed to a doctor. At first she was wary of my genteel manners and strange accent but a few trips to see the sights of London soon had her in the palm of my hand. It was a true love match.

We spent Christmas of 1891 together at the Sabbatini home and I can record it as the happiest and most blissful time of my life. Sometimes no words were spoken between Laura and myself, as to look upon each other was enough to reassure ourselves that a fire burned brightly in our hearts. We began to make plans for the future but inevitably some topics were best avoided on my part. How could I promise children? They may be diseased like their father and present defects at birth. How could I live alongside my bride without her detecting my morphine addiction? Surely that would lead to a torrent of questions and suppositions. However, I will tell you sincerely, no matter what dilemma arose, I wanted Laura to take me as her own and love me with tender care.

After a week of celebrations and general festivities, I returned to London to catch up with any correspondence that may be awaiting my attention and to read through the periodicals in case there was news on the 'Lambeth Mystery'.

Back in my lodgings at Lambeth Palace Road, I found a telegram from Daniel, my brother. It seemed that my family had sold my father's property and required me to attend to the legalities so that I may lawfully claim my share. That would mean a trip overseas. I was in two minds whether to go if I'm honest, on the one hand I would desperately miss Laura but on the other, additional funds would be mighty useful in planning our future together.

I informed my landlady of my intention to travel and once again secured my lodgings by paying her rent in advance. It was at this time that I was properly introduced to the other lodger at this address. His name was Walter Joseph Harper, a medical student and son of a prominent surgeon. He seemed a quiet lad, a little shy, but upon learning that we hailed from the same profession, we soon started up a hearty conversation. That was a most interesting parlez! As we fell into debate about the identity of the 'Lambeth Murderer', so too the discussion brushed upon the topic of a more heinous fiend, 'Jack the Ripper'. Now, with me being a trifle busy in 1888, I had missed the reports about those slaughtered prostitutes. This was certainly news of which I needed to hear more. It seemed there were five terrible crimes, perhaps even more could be attributed to brave 'Jack'. The dialogue continued for some time, mainly with me asking for details and either young Walter or Mrs. Sleaper filling me in.

What a lot I had missed in good old London town! Hard to take in the knowledge, that there was yet another fellow out there on a mission to depopulate the streets of whores. I had to smile, this had all the distinguishing traits of 'R'.

Now, I have to be careful dear reader, for although we have become well-acquainted, you and I, it is not good etiquette for me to speculate upon the deeds or misdeeds of my extraordinary chum 'R'. I will be so bold as to affirm that he, like myself, bore a deep hatred for the harlots earning their bread on the London streets. He also bore the affliction of a venereal disease, albeit far less debilitating than my own. We had become allies in the battle against whores but there was one other circumstance which had led us to bond.

Like my own most unfortunate predicament with Flora, my dear 'R' had also found himself on the receiving end of an unwanted pregnancy. And, likewise, 'R' had also been forced to marry the girl, afterwards bringing her to London to terminate the foetus. I will refrain from relating to you the outcome of 'R's escapades on that particular subject, but I do recall him becoming extremely bitter towards his new bride and events took a rather unsavory turn thereafter.

I must emphasize here that I had received little communication from him before my incarceration at Joliet, although I am certain that his intervention in my release came subtly via the British Consul's office. However, my attempts at locating him since my return to England, which I admit were rather feeble, had upturned nothing but rumors and a few unconfirmed sightings.

On January 6th 1892, I was back in Berkhampsted with Laura. It was to be a brief visit, as the following day I would take passage on the S.S. Sarnia. Oh, how she fussed about my luggage and sighed as I recounted how cold it would be in Canada. Laura made me promise that one day we would visit the land of my childhood together, a long honeymoon to meet my family perhaps. What pleasant thoughts. There was nothing I would like more than to knock on my brother's door with my elegant bride in tow, more than a match for his sour-faced bitch. Ha, ha, how proud I would be!

Despite my good spirits that day, I still had to think about the practicalities should something happen to me. There was always a chance that the police would catch my scent or that I would be tempted to take chances that would put me in unnecessary danger. Therefore I began to prepare.

That afternoon, with Mrs. Sabbatini's consent, Laura and I became engaged. I then put pen to paper and composed my Last Will and Testament, bequeathing all that I owned to my darling girl. I am sure that Laura found my actions quite farcical but I assured her that it was just a precaution should the ship go down or another such catastrophe. I gave her an address with which to correspond with me in Quebec and promised that I would be back as soon as my business was concluded.

You have no idea how hard it was to part from my beloved the next morning. There she stood upon the threshold, all teary faced and forlorn in her best satin gown, while I tied up the straps on my portmanteau and carefully checked the contents of my medical bag. I am not ashamed to say that I wish we had met at a different time, Laura and I. You see I still had a mission to accomplish, and complete it I would. That seed of destruction inside my brain was never going away, there would always be the crazy side of me. But Laura loved Dr. Neill, the respectable doctor who cared for his patients with tenderness and devotion. She had never met the other guy, Dr. Cream, the one who preyed on whores and lived a life of debauchery and crime. My poor darling, if only you knew, but nothing could change me. My past would always be there and that is exactly what forged my future.

Therefore I set off for Liverpool docks and my impending journey, elated that Laura had agreed to become my bride but downhearted that we would be separated for an almost immeasurable length of time.

Cast your mind back to my last sea voyage. Do you remember how I was tempted to get myself a little bitch to test my opiates on? That was such horseplay. I won't say that love had changed me, but I had mellowed a trifle at least and promised to keep my vials securely locked away, for the time being anyway. A shift had taken place within me, I could feel a certain tranquility as I dined and conversed with my fellow passengers. Perhaps it was the respectability that a forthcoming marriage brings to a chap or the drug of being in love. Whichever, I am sure that I presented myself as the most decent and honorable man aboard.

Beneath my stoic appearance the cogwheels in my head still turned with plans and connivances, that other side of me just yearning to eradicate more sluts and make a mark on the world. More deaths would happen, of that I was certain, but my darling Laura should not find out. If she even sensed a hint of betrayal, all would be lost.

I would somehow need to forge a plan whereby an arrest be made for the murder of Ellen Donworth, and maybe I could help the authorities by fingering the culprit.

Still in the back of my mind was the recent conversation between myself and the residents of 103 Lambeth Palace Road. The ghastly exploits of 'Jack the Ripper' four years previously was still very much an intense topic.

I did wonder why a fellow would go to all the trouble of ripping out a whore's innards but there would have been plenty of buyers I suppose. The East End hospitals were notoriously short of fresh specimens and we lived in a time when scrutiny into female genitalia was very much in vogue. Every doctor worth his salt wanted to come up with a cure for venereal disease, me included.

As my journey across the transatlantic progressed, so did my thoughts towards 'R'. We had conversed long into the night on many occasion, detailing plans on how London could have her streets cleansed for free. It would only take one discerning individual to make it his vocation in life to slay those filthy tarts one by one, deep in the backstreets away from the crowds. Had 'R' taken action, I pondered. I knew all too well of his leanings towards the arcane and remembered too his promises to a brotherhood far more powerful and notorious than either he nor I could ever hope to be.

12

Home of Rachel Cream, Quebec

It had been a long, long time since I had set eyes upon my sister, Rachel. Now a grown woman with a stubborn streak that my father would have been proud of, she welcomed me with open arms. Coming back to Canada had been the right decision, to be in the bosom of my family, if only until finances were agreed and my next course of action planned. The hardest part of returning was the way that everyone avoided the subject of my incarceration. I'd been locked away for ten years God Damn! Surely, you'd think they had something to ask me, at least to satisfy themselves of my innocence. But the silence said it all, even my own flesh and blood saw me as guilty, thank you folks, much appreciated! Only Rachel looked upon me with kindness, a raw sympathy in her eyes that told me she knew I had changed, I even suspect she knew I was ill. Didn't take much figuring out that she and Daniel had been deep in discussion about me, after I had left his house the previous summer.

My return to the fold didn't spark joy or celebrations, just a somber reflection upon our childhood and the parents we no longer had. I had always been my mother's son, whilst my brothers mirrored traits which were so definitely my father's. They had drive and ambition, I had pride and composure. It was I who had sat by my mother's side on her death bed, my brothers either at school or helping my father in the lumber yard, but Rachel had been there too, making broth and bringing cool compounds to ease our mother's suffering. Yes, Rachel had a good heart and she understood me more than any of my other siblings. When I told her of my new-found happiness, and my plans to bring Laura to Canada, she clasped my hand in genuine delight but there was still something, a deep furrow in her brow, that told me she suspected it may never be. We had no need to speak of her concerns, we both knew it would result in Rachel trying to coax me out of my criminal intentions, a fruitless task that would only lead to our estrangement. Whenever the topic touched on life in London I regaled my family with tales of medical dramas and West End theatre shows, not lies, but simply stories from my younger days.

My medication was never an issue in Canada, I ingested my drugs discreetly and if ever my sister did happen to enter a room as I measured out my dosage, it was always brushed off as a tonic for my weakened frame. I was a doctor, I could be trusted to prescribe my own remedy could I not? Nobody asked me what was wrong with me, I think they were afraid of what the answer might be. I was left to my own devices with no interrogation and no explanation. I can honestly swear that intervention from my family would not have swayed my reasoning one iota, that dark angel in my head was still there, whispering and plotting, ready to push the button when the next victim was ripe.

After impersonating the doting brother for a couple of weeks, my feet itched to escape and I headed west to Ontario where a stroke of genius would see my next plan come to fruition. I used the train journey as thinking time, considering all my options, and finally settling upon a drastic course of action.

I checked in to the swanky Metropole Hotel in London, just outside Ontario city, no particular reason for my choice, only perhaps that I had a penchant for places named London ha, ha! My idea was to convince residents of the hotel that Ellen Donworth's murderer was actually staying under the same roof as them, a ploy which I hoped would draw attention away from London, England and have the British police searching for their suspect in Canada. In turn, I reasoned, if their focus was across the Atlantic, I could slip back to England in the Spring and conduct my next abomination in peace. Rather clever don't you think?

Next, I ordered two hundred circulars to be printed with the words : ELLEN DONWORTH'S DEATH

'To the Guests of the Metrople Hotel

Ladies and Gentlemen, I hereby notify you that the person who poisoned Ellen Donworth on the 13th last October is today in the employ of the Metropole Hotel and that your lives are in danger as long as you remain in this Hotel.'

I signed the document W.H. Murray and dated it from London, April 1892. I then left instructions with the printer to distribute the leaflets in the Spring. Naturally I wanted to be well away from the scene before there was 'Mayhem at the Metropole'. All in all, I was quite proud of my clever plot.

Naturally it will have crossed your mind to question whether the English news would have been reported on those Trans-Atlantic shores, but let me put your mind at ease. You see, there was an almost fairytale idyll of London, and England, during those years, especially for those folks who had yet to experience her delights first hand. Canadians, and Americans alike, loved to read aloud the fantastical columns from that great British nation and then spend another hour in debate over breakfast discussing what was in vogue and which Lord had married beneath himself.

Even though the sinister events of the 'Jack the Ripper' murders were a full three years since, those foul crimes were still vivid in the minds of plenty. I would suppose it was due to the shear butcherous nature of Jack's methods that got those tongues wagging but the ingrained terror of the London underworld was not easily to be forgotten.

If I may be brutally honest with you friend, it was the fear in the hearts of those bitches that made my next steps easier. If I could be sure that the little sluts were trembling at the very thought of meeting their doom in those alleys and backstreets, it made my task more pleasurable. What kind of fiend would I be if my prey were relaxed and unsuspecting? The combination of being both infallible an unscrupulous was the very nature of my game. And I was smarter than Jack, for the harlots would open their doors and let me in to their homes.

I stayed a couple of weeks in Ontario and tarried back and forth to the lawyer's office where my father's estate was being divided. As the eldest son, I had already received the largest part of my inheritance, that had been my means to move to England after Joliet, but I still expected another healthy windfall to come my way. As it was, after taxes and duties, my siblings and I received $1,400 each, a rather paltry sum in my estimation but still it would be enough to top up my already healthy bank balance and start my married life in London.

I confess my friend, I have always been extravagant when it comes to elegant clothes and fine dining and the rustle of notes in my pocket did nothing to dull my expensive tastes. I ate the juiciest steaks in town, drank the most full-bodied French wine on offer and ordered myself a cashmere coat, the likes of which would bring envy to all those who cast eyes upon me. Elated at my carefree lifestyle and buoyed by the prospect of marrying Laura, I should have felt like the luckiest man alive but a dark cloud hung over me like the shadow of Satan himself.

It was the sleepless nights and constant roar in my head that dampened my mood. By now I had doubled my intake of morphine and added various other opiates to the mix to create a precarious cocktail that both numbed my senses and gave me a constant high. Even so, slumber evaded me and I felt both exhausted and cranky. The only thing that ever lifted my spirits for a reasonable length of time was the killing. There had only been two London deaths so far but the intoxicating sensations that I experienced both times was enough to convince me that I need to continue my quest.

In the second week of March 1892, I visited my sister for the last time. Daniel had arrived the night before as he too wanted to bid me farewell. It was almost as though my brother and sister had received a premonition that day, telling them that this would be my final curtain call. Rachel made me promise that should I ever need her, for anything at all, she would come to England to be with me. Her sentiments were rather overwhelming, causing me to realize that my appearance must have deteriorated so much that my family thought I was at death's door. I left soon after, feeling no remorse for my actions, only pity for my family.

On 23rd March I sailed aboard the Britannic to Liverpool docks once again. Are you waiting with baited breath dear reader, to discover some fellow passenger displaying the symptoms of poison from my vials? Ha, ha, you misjudge me. I was in need on conserving my energy for the main event you see, plotting and scheming drains a chap to the point of exhaustion. There was arduous labor ahead of me in those ungodly Lambeth streets, so much to do and such caution to be taken.

And so, should you happen to glimpse the veritable Dr. Neill aboard that liner, you would have seen charm, impeccable manners and a wit to challenge many a jester.

Not more than three or four evenings had passed before the invitations to dine in the company of this fellow or that came to my cabin door. I was flattered but not surprised. Who wouldn't covet the presence of the charismatic doctor? Despite the gay evenings, my days were less than jovial. Copious amounts of wine infused with my usual concoction of opiates left me lethargic and tense. The pain in my head thundered on, like a constant torrent of water racing to the falls, whilst my joints cracked under each new attempt to seek comfort on the mattress beneath me. Those days were long, there was little to occupy my wandering mind and my thoughts naturally turned towards Laura. How long would it be until the time was right to put a ring on her finger and lead her to our bedchamber, I mused. Be patient, I told myself then, there is still work to be done.

Slightly rested after an uneventful journey, I travelled down to London and took a room at Edward's Hotel in Euston Square.

Now you may be wondering my dear friend, why did I spend good banknotes on a swanky room when I had my own lodgings just a few miles away? There is no more mystery to my actions than the fact that I needed some carnal interaction that night, it would put me in the mood for my next victim and relieve the tension from my loins. I can almost hear you cry, 'What about your poor fiancee?'. Well, we hadn't actually got around to exploring each other sexually you see, I wanted my bride to be a pure flower on our wedding night, that would be the ultimate pleasure. But a man has his needs and if it meant a quick tussle with an uninhibited whore, then so be it. I am not a heartless man, but I fully believe that what the eye doesn't see, the heart won't bleed for.

And so, a couple of hours after my arrival, I had selected a suitable bedding partner and took her up to my room for an evening of erotic entertainment. Afterwards I had no thoughts of doing away with her, can't even remember her name, but it sure did put me in the mood for another poisoning. I just needed a few days of careful preparation.

It was also time to see Laura. I headed down to Berkhampsted with a spring in my step, laden with gifts for my darling girl but determined to make my visit brief as I needed to get back to work as soon as possible. It had been too long since Matilda Clover's passing and my urges could not be kept under control for long, I might even try to make it a double hit next time!

Laura was overjoyed to see me, throwing herself into my arms before I had even removed my overcoat. She talked incessantly about her new dress designs, showing me page after page of sketches and asking when we would set a date to be married so that she could move to London to fulfill her dream of becoming dressmaker to the city socialites.

'All in good time' I promised her. The best laid plans are those that are prepared carefully. Besides, I couldn't have her on my doorstep until I had figured out a way to conduct my business without arousing her suspicion.

As I scoured the newspapers for mention of a murder suspect at the Metropole Hotel in Canada (those circulars should have been causing alarm amongst the guests by now) frustration began to set in. There was nothing. No special forces to be dispatched across the Atlantic, no arrests made, not one scrap of journalistic revelation to cause a stir. I would have to take further action, there was no other way forward.

That is where I enlisted the assistance of Laura. Under my careful dictation, I had her write two letters. One, to a certain Countess Russell, residing at the Savoy Hotel, which accused her husband of poisoning Ellen Donworth. Don't ask me why I should choose such a prominent lady, only that I had seen mention of her in the Society pages and figured she was as good a target as anyone. The second letter was to a surgeon by the name Dr. William Henry Broadbent, declaring that I knew of his involvement in the crime. Of course I had no wish to incriminate myself, so asked Laura to sign the letters 'M. Malone'. Hopefully they would cause enough of a stir to have the bobbies on high alert.

Of course Laura questioned me on both accounts. What kind of malarkey was I involved in, she wanted to know. You know they say 'Love is blind'? Well my friend, in Laura's case it was positively destitute of vision! I was writing on behalf of a friend who knew all the details of these horrible acts, I told her. And do you know what? She believed me. It took very little persuasion to convince her that I was acting in my 'friend's' best interests, and that all we intended to do was bring this vile perpetrator to justice. What an honest and upright citizen her beloved Dr. Neill was! How thoughtful to act upon his pal's suspicions. I smiled, darling girl you know nothing of who I am and what I do. I am your finest dream and worst nightmare, don't attempt to scratch my surface.

13

Back in Lambeth

By the 9th April 1892, I was comfortably settled back in to my lodgings in Lambeth and more than ready to start work. I decided to try a different patch that night and wandered the streets around Piccadilly. I was later than usual going out that evening, having firstly wanted to pen a letter to Laura explaining that I might be busy at the hospital for a couple of weeks, and the streets were busy with all manner of toffs and wenches going about their business. Approaching St. James's Hall I spotted the perfect catch. A rather voluptuous woman, with large pendulous breasts and a look of knowledge about her that only comes from years of experience on the streets. She would do perfectly. Ha, ha, hello number three!

The gal quickly introduced herself as Lou Harvey, I'm guessing it would be short for Louisa, and explained that we would have to find a place to go as her own home was across the city in St. John's Wood. Now you know dear reader, I don't have a problem spending my money, especially when the end result will give me so much satisfaction, so we walked along to the Palace Hotel in Garrick Street and I secured us a room for the night.

You will remember that I like to give these bitches a little treat in their final hours, so we dined in the hotel restaurant and became acquainted over a bottle of burgundy. Lou was a fine woman of the night, she knew all kinds of tricks and when morning dawned I had a wide grin of satisfaction upon my face. Now my friend, although I fully intended to poison the whore, I concluded that to do away with her in the hotel room would be rather indiscreet, especially in light of the fact that a good number of residents had cast their eyes upon us the night before as we dined and chattered like a pair of newlyweds. Therefore, it was agreed that we would meet that very evening at Charing Cross Station. I felt not a shadow of a doubt that Lou would be there, as I had promised to gift her some pills which would give a beautiful blush to her pale complexion.

And so it was, at the exact appointed hour, Lou Harvey was waiting for me. These strumpets really are too easy to coax aren't they? Of course, I couldn't just give her the pills and run away could I? That's really not my style. So we walked arm in arm to the Northumberland Public House where we partook of a glass of wine, and then strolled back along the Embankment. It was only then that I offered her my specially concocted capsules and, as far as I could tell at that point, the dumb bitch swallowed them. Knowing that the toxins would take effect within the hour, I then made an excuse to leave. I was a busy doctor after all, needed to attend to all matter of important consultations! I assured Miss Harvey that I would meet her again at 11pm, a promise that I had no intention of fulfilling. I mean, what would be the point? By that hour she would be on her way to the mortuary, ha ha!

The euphoria of knowing I had eradicated another whore spurred me on. I returned to my room and ingested a larger than usual dose of morphine, followed by a pinch of cocaine. Together the drugs gave me energy and drive, putting me in the right frame of mind to go hunting again. I spent most of that night measuring out strychnine and filling some gelatin capsules in which to administer them. I worked tirelessly, plotting and making notes in my journal, only resting for a couple of hours the next day before preparing to hit the streets once again.

That afternoon I occupied myself with sketching a rough plan of the pathways around me. I had gradually come to know the immediate vicinity of Lambeth, a sheer warren of alleys, open thoroughfares and secluded yards, but eventually the need to broaden my hunting ground would arise. For that occasion a chap should be ready with an escape route should he need to withdraw in haste.

Once my map was completed to a reasonable degree of satisfaction, I carefully opened my dutiful medicine case and took stock of the contents inside. Numerous vials still remained unopened – camomile, dove powder, cannabis and more. These were the drugs of my regular trade, not to be casually wasted on some penny whore. The precious stock with seals intact were to serve a covetable purpose in my future career. You see, I figured that with a wife to support, it would be paramount that I create more of my sensational elixirs to serve up to the general public of London. If my previous success could be measured in English pounds, I was assured a most comfortable future. Whether it be epilepsy or the pox, there was plentiful suffering all around me and those wretches would be more than happy to cross my palm with silver in return for salvation. If only I could guarantee that my other, less virtuous, escapades could be kept under control, well then both Laura and London would be safe.

That night was pretty dismal. In between lashings of rain the wind howled through the alleyways like a rampant wolf in search of its prey. Or just like me, perhaps! This time I decided to stay on familiar territory and loitered around the dingy buildings of Stamford Street. In truth I hoped to meet Liz Masters, remember my first conquest in London? It would be easy with her, she already knew me and would be glad to accept my miraculous potion. As it turned out Liz must have been elsewhere that night, but luck was on my side and two naive looking girls sauntered my way just as I was about to give up hope and return home. How convenient, they lived right there at Number 118, both of them! What fortune!

I told you I was ready for a double murder, and yes siree, I certainly was. Of course, that would be after I had enjoyed the twofold offerings of these nubile greenhorns. I'm sure you can use your imagination to recreate the scene my friend, let's just say whatever scenario you dream up you couldn't be far off the mark in my dalliances that night!

What good hosts these girls were too. After finishing our business, they offered to share a supper of malt beer and canned salmon, the perfect way to help down the pills that I now offered. This time I explained that the little cachous would stave off the dreaded disease that so many London street-walkers feared. What perfect patients they were, tossing back the capsules like their lives depended upon it. Of course their lives, and deaths, did depend upon it, ha, ha!

On parting I promised to meet them again, but we both know that the only way I would lay eyes upon these two sluts again were should I happen to gain employment at the local emergency room. Oh, it felt good, another two to be chalked up on my scoreboard. I was first-rate, and the fun had only just begun!

This time the newspapers took the double poisoning as a serious case of homicide. 'Lambeth Poisoner loose on the streets of London' the headlines warned. Hum, satisfaction at last. At least now I was being recognized for my efforts.

Despite the initial reports, the days dragged on with still no suspect list or hypothetical theories. I scoured the periodicals daily but as days turned in to weeks the story moved from the front page to the second, third and then finally occupied the tiniest column half way in.

My quill poised, I set upon a wonderful task of penmanship that should put both my shy young co-lodger, Walter Harper, and his eminent father Joseph in the frame for the murders in Stamford Street. This seemed to rouse the journalists from their premature slumber and soon the cogs of the rumor mill were turning fiercely once more. Of course poor Walter had no idea that, as I tipped my hat at him when we passed on the stairs, I was also plotting to seal his fate. To all who met me I was the respectable Dr. Neill, perfect tenant, professional medic and concerned citizen. If only they knew!

One such gentleman who appreciated my candid and friendly conversation was a chap I met at Armstead's Photo Studio when I went to get a portrait photograph taken as a token gift for Laura. John Haynes was a former detective from New York and now rented rooms upstairs from the studio. He was an extremely likeable fellow, there was something forthright and no-nonsense in his nature.

Both being familiar with American territory, we struck up a dialogue almost immediately and the most topical thread at that time was of course the Stamford Street murders. Being on first-rate terms with the law, John was interested to ask my expertise on poisons and autopsies, an opinion on which I was delighted to oblige, and we were soon sharing supper whilst discussing the recent atrocities.

I perhaps may have ingested too much wine one evening when dining with John, and certainly felt my tongue running away with itself, as I recounted some little known facts and then tripped myself up by mentioning Matilda Clover and Lou Harvey. You see, up to that point, there had been no tabloid mention of Miss. Harvey and my new friend listened with earnest as he jotted down this new information. I think I even erroneously pointed out Matilda Clover's door as we passed by on our journey homeward.

Little did I know that my new-found buddy was also great pals with an Inspector at Scotland Yard. This new liaison was to become my undoing. You see unbeknown to me, a deep suspicion had arisen in John Haynes' mind and I had obviously given away too many details for him to believe I was just spouting my own theories. Behind the scenes, a thick web was encircling this particular spider and I had no idea how to crawl my way out of it.

As I went about my daily business, so too did the local police. I innocently visited my regular haunts and tried my utmost to carry on as though nothing were happening.

I could feel the net closing in and would regularly catch glimpses of plain clothed detectives following me as I left my lodging house. They wouldn't catch me up to my tricks this time though. I avoided all contact with the seedier goods on offer in the city and held my head up like the perfect gent.

The permanent presence of spies all around me did nothing to deter me from my endeavors. Of course it caused frustrating delays in executing my plans but I felt convinced that eventually the detectives would realize their mission to be fruitless and move on to more lucrative business elsewhere. It was all a game to me. Instead of whiling away the hours in my meagre lodgings, I taunted those pursuing me with a game of cat and mouse. Each morning I would settle upon a different route and wander the city at leisure, sometimes quickening my pace, then slowing to a shuffle, all for the pleasure of catching the shadows of those employed to tail me.

I led them a merry dance, I can tell you. One fine day I would be leaping up the steps of St. Thomas's hospital, spending an hour in conversation with the duty clerk under pretense of seeking employment, the next I could be found simply standing on Waterloo Bridge waiting for the moon to rise. Come rain or shine I ventured out relentlessly, taking a bite of lunch here or lingering over coffee there. Wherever my tread, the tip-tapping of footsteps at my rear could always be faintly heard. On particularly wet days, the young constables in pursuit would be so bold as to enter the taverns where I supped. They made no sham of mingling with the crowd and eyed me suspiciously as I tucked myself in to a narrow corner booth. What games friend! But despite the lack of evidence for my crimes, those bastards never tired of hounding me.

Later I was to discover that during this relatively quiet period of surveillance, the London police had been doing a spot of work with forces overseas and now had a very clear picture of my true identity. They knew my real name, all about my incarceration at Joliet and worst of all they knew about Laura.

Whilst I cautiously tore pages from my journal, most importantly those that detailed the whores I had struck off, samples of my handwriting had already been gathered in the case against me. Every blackmail letter, every note, and even my Canadian passport were to feature in the case against me.

The final straw would come when the authorities finally took heed of what I had written months before, and deemed it the right time to exhume Matilda Clover's body.

At 5.25pm on 3rd June 1892 I was confronted in Lambeth Palace Road, by Inspector Tonbridge, who put me under arrest. I assured the officer that it was a case of mistaken identity and he was pursuing the wrong fellow, but he wouldn't listen. At first I was booked in to Bow Street Police Station, a drab grey building full of drunkards and thieves. The only consolation being that I had a cell to myself in which to think out my plea.

The only charge they could possibly bring against me at this stage was blackmail, but alas, it wasn't long before the autopsy had been performed upon Clover's rotting corpse. Within a few days the charge had been changed to one of murder with the inquest jury casting their verdict:

'We are unanimously agreed that Matilda Clover died of strychnine poisoning and that the poison was administered by Thomas Neill with intent to destroy life'.

That night was a sleepless frenzy of quick-thinking and frustration. Now that I had been caught I had to talk my way out of this diabolical situation. What about my plans to marry Laura? What about the money I had stashed away for our future together? Who did I know in London that could come to my rescue? Where the hell was 'R' when I needed him? The only way to go was to maintain that I was innocent until it would hold its worth no longer.

14

Holloway Prison, London

As soon as I had been formerly charged at Bow Street, I was transferred to the steel fortress of Holloway. You may imagine that by this time I would be in the grip of fear, or an intense panic, but you would be wrong. My utmost concern at that point was to get a message, via my lawyer Mr. Waters, to Laura explaining that these buffoons had arrested the wrong man and that she should not worry as all would be well.

I must say I was rather concerned as to how things were panning out but I was not going to lose my nerve unduly as there was every chance I would be released at any time. Therefore, I made up my mind to stoically bear the daily grind inside the prison walls until the day came that I had to face judge and jury. Those were the longest months of my life, I can tell you.

There was little difference between the dark cells in Joliet and the slate colored rooms that made up Holloway. It gave me a sense of deja-vu, but also the strong mind to face each day as it came. Mr. Waters followed my instructions and sent a telegram to Rachel asking her to come. He also mailed my letter to Laura, begging her to believe in my innocence. For Rachel, I had a long wait as she boarded a passenger ship from New York, taking weeks to reach the English shores. Laura wrote to me within the week, explaining that she would stand by me but could not come as she was to stand up in court as witness for the prosecution! How my heart bled at those words, they were asking my darling girl to take oath against me! My lawyer explained that Laura's handwriting had been submitted as evidence that she wrote two of the blackmail letters. Of course, she had innocently recounted my tale of simply wishing to help a friend in need and had thereby implicated herself in my plan.

As the weeks passed so my health deteriorated. It was a direct result of me not being able to regulate my medication. My appetite was the first part of me to diminish, followed by urgent bowel movements and then the blinding migraines that I had always fought to control. I knew then that I had reached the peak of my illness. One blessing as a consequence of my condition was being formally excused from labor and given a cell by myself close to the infirmary. The weeks passed and I was still no farther along the path of securing my freedom. I began to get agitated.

On 16th August 1892, I summoned all of my courage and wrote another letter to Laura. This time I outlined the lies told by Inspector Tonbridge and his wretched colleagues. I emphasized the positives : Lucy Rose the servant residing at Matilda Clover's lodgings had failed to positively identify me as the man she had seen on the stairs, and the man who saw 'a gent' leaving Shrivell and Marsh's residence refused to say it was me. There was still hope that I would be freed. In reply, Laura was sweet and caring but I could feel doubt creeping in to her sentences. I could see tiny circles where the ink had smudged from her tears, and she had omitted to use her pet name for me. Had she lost faith?

At last Rachel arrived, fresh-faced from her journey and determined to have me tell her the truth. It was not in my nature to plead guilty, in my eyes I had simply been doing a duty for my fellow citizens, by cleansing their streets of a terrible disease. Therefore, I pleaded innocence of all charges. Rachel looked me in the eyes and told me she knew what I had done. She could feel the evil lurking within me but still she promised to stand by my side. After all, we were family were we not? She also pledged to speak with Laura, not only to satisfy herself that I had chosen a pure sweetheart, but also to try to keep Laura's spirits up on my behalf.

The weeks turned in to months and finally Mr. Waters came with the news that my trial was set for 17th October. Rachel brought me clothes to wear in court, so that I may hold my head high when facing the prosecution, even though I was to be manacled by the wrists throughout.

It was so very hard to hear my sweet Laura recount how I had asked her to write those wretched letters. She believed in me, she said, I had only been helping a friend. But innocent though she believed me to be, she was unable to look me in the eyes. That was when my heart broke in two.

I was also unprepared for the trail of witnesses that traipsed in and out of that courtroom over the next five days. There was Emily Sleaper my landlady's daughter, John Haynes my new American friend, Kirkby the chemist assistant from whom I had purchased strychnine, and even the lovely Liz Masters took the stand to testify how she had been watching out for me at the appointed time and seen me with Matilda Clover. The biggest shock of all was when Lou Harvey came sauntering through with the bailiff. She was supposed to be six feet under! Turns out that clever bitch had thrown my pills over the side at the Embankment, sealing my fate to be sure.

With such an array of testimony against me, it is no wonder that the judge pronounced me guilty and instead of returning me to my dark cell in Holloway, I was at once transferred to the confines of Newgate. But honestly friend, by that time I was so resigned to my fate that it felt like a release to know that it was all over. I never did believe that they would hang me though. I truly thought that I would either stand for retrial and be acquitted or serve a five to six year stretch before having my sentence commuted as before. I returned to my cell no more distressed than before the trial but convincing myself that there would be a reprieve coming shortly. Day after day I waited, but no news.

Finally Mr. Waters told me straight, no last minute stay of execution, no pardon. I was to hang at Newgate gaol.

Do not waste your tears on me my friend, for I can bear my punishment. There were worse night tremors during my sleeping hours than those I would face on the gallows. My only wish was that I could die a happy man, having known the tender touch of my beloved Laura, but my little girl was lost to me now.

Rachel sat with me every day until the time came for me to face my maker. She would read passages from the bible and sing softly to try to soothe my pounding head.

By now three weeks had passed since judgment day and with each new sunrise I hoped that my beloved girl would come to me in my final hours. As each evening drew to a close, I knew that my wait had been in vain, I knew that Laura was not coming. I knew that she had deserted me. We would never be together now, she was just like the rest of them, selfish and uncaring. Therefore, I summoned Mr. Waters and arranged to change my Last Will and Testament. I would leave everything I had to my family, the bulk of it going to my dearest sister Rachel. Laura would never have her fashion empire, well not with my money anyway, she had forsaken me in my hour of need.

On 15th November 1892, the night before I was to be hanged, the chaplain came to say prayers and asked if I had a final confession. I had nothing to say. What could I say dear reader? I sought no spiritual counsel as I had nothing to regret. My deeds had been carried out in good faith. Before retiring to my bed for one last sleepless night, Rachel came to me to say goodbye. The telltale red rims around her eyes said it all, she could not bring herself to forgive me but she did hope that the Lord would give me a second chance and let me in to Heaven where I could toil away my sins. We hugged one last time, only the rustle of taffeta on her dress giving any indication that there were mortals in that deathly cell, and parting in silence she was gone.

My final meal came, but my stomach was still frail and I ate but a few morsels. I thanked the wardens heartily however, they had provided a fine supper given the location and circumstances. In another era I would have these chaps for my alliances any day. As midnight drew near, a note was hurriedly passed through the bars and I strained to read the words by light of the moon. Was it from Laura? Had she found it in her heart to pledge her love to me after all?

I slowly read the words, adjusting my glasses carefully.

It was from 'R'. He had read about my plight and wished to send his condolences. He could not come in person, he said, there were circumstances which would put him in jeopardy should he be seen within the city. I smiled, more women trouble I supposed, he always was a ladies man. It was signed with a handsome flourish and the words 'Well Done' at the bottom. He understood me, 'R' knew what my mission had stood for, and me his. Now I truly knew, I would take his secret to the grave.

The window in my cell was too high for me to see out but, early next morning as I paced my eight foot room, I could hear the dull roar of the crowd as they gathered outside to hear me swing. I could just make out the words 'Lambeth Poisoner' and 'Murderer'. That made me smile, at least they had come to the right show. A burdensome weight had lifted from my shoulders. I no longer had to pretend. I could look folks straight in the eye and say 'Yes, you know what, I did it". There would be no more pretending to be an upright citizen, no more perfect fiancé, no kindly doctor Cream. I could hold my head up and say, 'This is the real me'.

Are you coming with me friend? To stand upon those gallows where the hangman awaits his prize? It takes a brave man to walk that last passageway without trembling knees and his bladder threatening to burst. Take each step with pride, put one foot in front of the other just as though you were walking to your own front door. Do not be afraid, that motley crew cannot see us, there is only the Governor, the chaplain, a warden, one police constable and Mr. Billington the hangman. All the good people of London are outside the walls and will only know I have gone by the raising of the black flag. Let them shout, for they will not have the satisfaction of glimpsing my face in these final moments.

The warden looks me in the eye and asks, 'Any final words?'. I think. I have nothing to disclose, all the dirty laundry I had was aired in that courtroom, there is nothing else. Do I have any last words for Laura? No. Despite the hole in my heart where her love used to reside, I have nothing to say. She did not come, therefore we are lovers no more. Can I think of one good friend with whom I have shared a dozen laughs and more escapades than you will know? Oh yes, of course there is someone, and so, finally I mutter 'Goodbye Jack'.

Now here is the hood, placed carefully over my head. It smells of something musty and herbal, could it be lavender or do I just imagine that? Could it be that my senses have parted company with my brain and I sense the fragrant smells of toilet water that Laura would dab upon her dainty white wrists. How foolish of me, of course she is not here.

Now something heavy, a rope looped carefully to make a noose around my neck. My, how time has slowed and every second feeling like an hour. Are you with me dear reader? Are you still here? Do not let me face this alone, stay with me until it is over, take a deep breath and follow me to the grave.

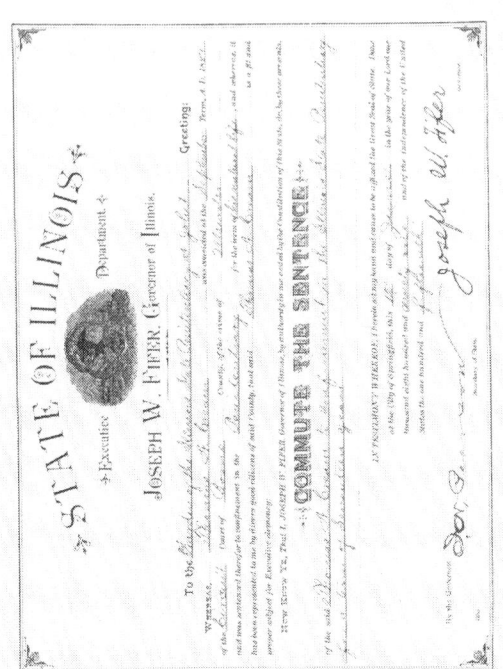

COMMUTATION OF SENTENCE 1891
ILLINOIS STATE ARCHIVES

UNDATED IMAGE OF CREAM (ESTIMATED 1892)
SCIENCE MUSEUM

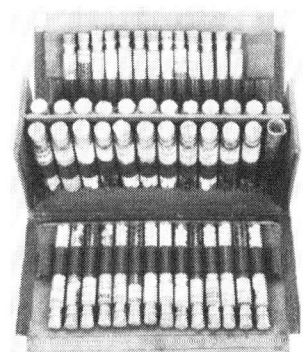

CREAM'S MEDICAL BAG 1892
CRIME MUSEUM, SCOTLAND YARD

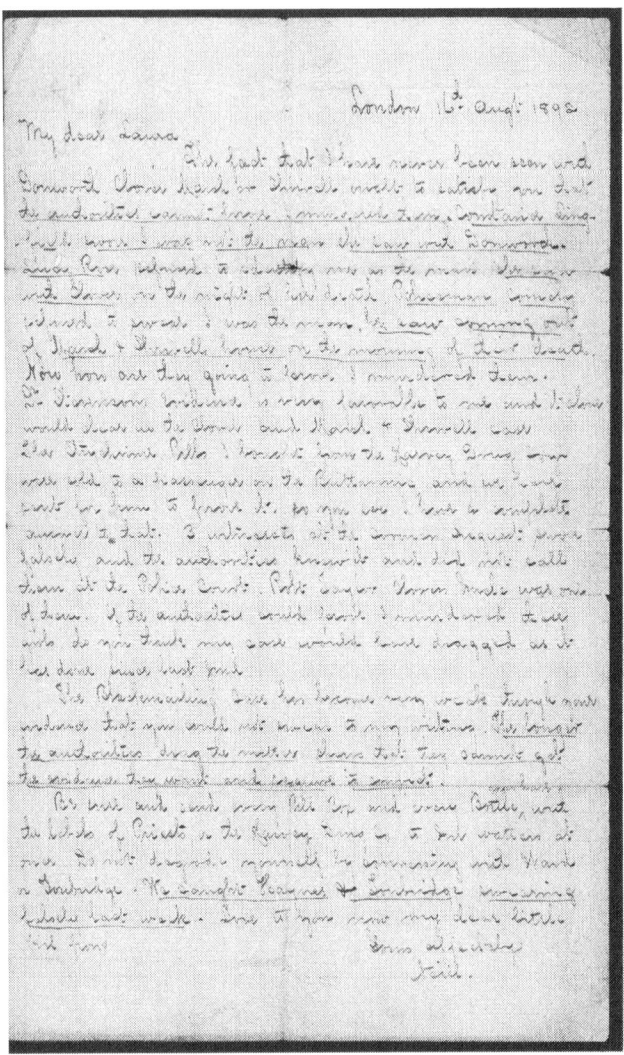

LETTER FROM CREAM WRITTEN IN CUSTODY 1892
SCIENCE MUSEUM

15

My Dearest Reader

Now is the time for us to say goodbye. We have traveled a long and somewhat bumpy road together, you and I. You have seen me at my very best, and then turned the pages to catch me at my worst. Do you understand me now? I fear not, but at least I can hope that the glimpses of my life that I have given to you will be enough to hold strong in your memory until you go to your grave.

I did not ask for forgiveness in my final hours, just as now I do not ask you to forgive me. Please just accept me for what I have done and try to find it in your heart to understand why I had to take those fateful steps. I am a man of passion, intelligence and conviction: do not hold it against me. As for my good friend 'R', I am sure that one day he too will share his story with you.

You now hold a secret. You know my whereabouts in 1888, the year of those fateful Ripper murders, something which can be proven beyond all reasonable doubt. Do what you will with that knowledge, then let me rest in peace. Do not be afraid to share what I have confided in you, after all we are friends, are we not?

Yours Respectfully

Thomas

About the Author

Having been brought up in a small village in the English countryside, A.J.Griffiths-Jones has plenty of happy memories from which to source information for her novels. However, it's been a long journey. Spanning three decades and two continents, her career & personal life have taken some incredible turns, finally bringing A.J. back to her roots and a promising writing career.

As a young woman, A.J. left the rolling Shropshire hills behind her & headed to London, where she became fascinated in the world of Victorian crime & in particular the unsolved case of 'Jack the Ripper'. Having read every book available to her on the subject, she started her own mini investigation which eventually led to her first non-fiction publication. However, there was a long period of research necessary before A.J. could finally complete her first book and during the intervening years she relocated to China with her husband and took up a post as Language Training Manager for an International bank. As the need for English grew within the company, A.J's responsibilities expanded until she was liasing between two cities and nearly three thousand employees. An initial two year move soon turned into a decade and the couple found themselves in the vast metropolis of Shanghai for a much longer period than they had firstly intended.

Using their Asian home as a base, A.J. and her better half travelled extensively during their time overseas, visiting New Zealand, Australia, Philippines, Malaysia, Thailand and many provinces within China itself At weekends they would jump into their Jeep and set off to remote villages and mountains, armed with little more than a compass and a map set in Chinese characters, photographing their trip as they explored. Eventually the desire to move back to the U.K. prevailed and the couple returned to their native land in 2012. It was at this point that A.J. made the decision to fulfill her lifetime ambition of becoming an author.

Initially embarking on penmanship in the historical crime genre, A.J. felt it necessary to create a balance between research and writing. The long hours of studying census reports and old newspapers were beginning to take their toll and, having a natural ability to see the funny side of everything, she decided to turn her hand to writing suspense novels with a comical twist. This newfound combination of writing styles has enabled A.J. to get the best of both worlds. For half of her working week she creates humorous characters in idyllic locations, whilst the rest of her hours are devoted to research in the Victorian era.

In her free time, A.J.Griffiths-Jones is a keen gardener, growing her own produce and creating unique recipes which she regularly cooks for friends & family. Her plan is to create healthy, filling meals which will eventually be compiled into a cookbook. In her free time A.J. still enjoys travelling, although these days she spends her time visiting Europe and the British Isles, and takes regular holidays in Turkey where she has a relaxing holiday home, which also serves as a haven to complete the final chapters in her books with a glass of wine and a beautiful sunset.

Another of the author's passion's is reading, especially books that take her out of her comfort zone and into a different historical period.

Nowadays, A.J. lives in a Shropshire market town with her husband and beloved Chinese cat, Humphrey. She regularly gives talks at local venues and has also appeared as a guest speaker at New Scotland Yard, where her investigative research was well-received by the Metropolitan Police Historical Society. The author's professional plan is to write a series of suspense novels as well as non-fiction publications relating to notorious historical figures.

Printed in Great Britain
by Amazon